CAJUN PIG

BOUCHERIES, COCHON DE LAITS AND BOUDIN

DIXIE POCHÉ
FOREWORD BY CHEF JOHN D. FOLSE

AMERICAN PALATE

Published by American Palate
A Division of The History Press
Charleston, SC
www.historypress.com

First published 2020

Manufactured in the United States

ISBN 9781467144469

Library of Congress Control Number: 2020941803

Dedicated to my sisters, Ginger and Maxine, for memories of barefoot summers and Sunday afternoons at the Old Place.

CONTENTS

FOREWORD

There's a saying in the old African American churches of Louisiana that once the congregation has contributed to the collection plate, a preacher dissatisfied with the offering might encourage greater donations by saying, "Thank y'all so much for bringing me the pig tails and feet, but we need to get a little higher up on that hog." As Louisianans, we tend to dine "higher up on that hog" with every outdoor food function and meal we eat.

We're blessed in Louisiana. Our temperate weather and rich, alluvial soil allow us three great growing seasons. Wild game is abundant—from white-tailed deer to land birds and migratory waterfowl. The waters of the Gulf Coast teem with fresh shrimp, oysters, crabs and finfish. And it really doesn't matter who's cooking. Grant it, Mamère's cooking is hard to beat, but the roadside cafés serve great étouffée and gumbo, too. Pull into any gas station, and you're sure to find delicious boudin, boudin balls and crispy cracklings to die for. Then, there are our outdoor food feasts—crawfish boils, shrimp and crab cookouts, fish fries, cochon de laits and boucheries. It's the pork-related cuisine that St. Martin Parish native Dixie Poché finds so fascinating.

In 2016, I was inspired to preserve the tradition of the boucherie by hosting one at my White Oak Estate & Gardens in Baton Rouge. Louisiana Public Broadcasting stepped in to document the harvesting, cooking and camaraderie associated with this living Louisiana tradition. We *passed such a good time* that we made it an annual outdoor gathering every February. That's where I met Dixie, who hobnobbed with the butchers and chefs demonstrating the art of preparing Cajun delicacies such as hog's head cheese, andouille, boudin, maudlin, crackling and other "Spoils of the Boucherie."

Dixie elucidates on a variety of topics in her book from the arrival and history of the pig in Louisiana to traditional recipes. She discusses Louisiana boucheries alongside similar pig-related celebrations of other regions. Her text covers many of the pork festivals that are held yearly throughout the state, such as the Boudin Festival in Scott and the Swine Festival in Basile. But what wins my heart—and stomach—is Dixie's inclusion of popular grocery stores and specialty meat markets in the heart of Cajun country. For those not yet indoctrinated into the food ways of Louisiana, she carefully defines some of our favorite Cajun pork dishes.

Cajun Pig is a tremendous resource tool that is seasoned with great historic photographs as well. When it comes to swining and dining in Louisiana, Dixie Poché has it covered. From snout to tail—it's all here!

—Chef John D. Folse, CEC, AAC
Louisiana's "Culinary Ambassador to the World"
Gonzales, Louisiana

ACKNOWLEDGEMENTS

I t's been an eye-opening experience for me to attend a pig roast as I peer eye-to-eye with a roasted pig with an apple in its mouth. From a distance, I saw chefs stirring what I mistakenly believed to be chocolate pudding in a bowl. It was actually pig blood; the chefs were preparing blood boudin.

I enjoyed many one-of-a-kind experiences as I jumped in the car to travel through South Louisiana to dance to zydeco music and hunt for mom-and-pop shops to sample an endless array of boudin balls or pickled pig lips. And those were just the appetizers! The heartwarming stories shared by shop owners and chefs reminded me of my aunt and uncle who ran a meat market in St. Martin Parish. I admired their dedication to customers along with the mouth-watering dishes of their Sunday plate lunches.

Thanks to Chef John Folse for setting the stage for so many writers and chefs. He has a vast knowledge of Cajun history, and I am appreciative of his assistance. It was through his annual Fete de Bouchers that my interest in writing about boucheries was sparked.

I am grateful for the hospitality shown to me by the Henry family in Mermentau Cove. Their Beau Chenes farm was a perfect venue for hosting the Cadien Toujours Boucherie. This organization and the efforts behind it to share Cajun traditions are admirable.

Thanks to Joan Kaiser Bergeaux of Krotz Springs for spending so much time with me sharing the amazing Orphan Train story of her grandparents.

Small general store, Jeanerette, Louisiana, 1938. *New York Public Library*.

Finally, a very special *merci* to photographer/French teacher/Cajun cook/cousin/friend Annette Huval for rising at rooster's crow to attend piggy events and shoot amazing photos that tell the delightful story of old-fashioned Cajun gatherings.

ROAD TRIPPIN' IN THE SOUTH

If you come to a fork in the road, take it.
—Yogi Berra

Discovering a diamond in the rough for dining out has always been a beloved pastime of mine. I'm searching for something cozy like Grandma's house where each table is topped with vintage salt and pepper shakers. Knickknacks are scattered on shelves. Autographed photos of celebrities who have stopped by to dine adorn the walls. I hop up to an empty seat at a well-worn lunch counter, perfectly placed for people watching while listening to local chatter. A cheery waitress asks me how my day is going and recites the blue plate special. When an eatery has been in the same family for years and they are excited to share their stories, I know I have opened a treasure box.

Fresh wildflowers in mason jars, cloth napkins folded on dining tables, aroma of food simmering in the kitchen and mismatched dining chairs are all eye-catching. The creativity of the plating and layers of seasoning of the plated dishes say a lot too. Are there unusual dishes on the menu? Although squirrel sauce piquante is a camp-style Cajun delicacy, you won't find it on too many menus.

My curiosity for trying out new places began when my family and I enjoyed road trips during childhood summer breaks. When we were hungry and ready to chow down, it was rare that we picked up fast food. Rather, we chose a ramshackle barn-like building located on a back road. Off-the-

Pontachoula, Louisiana roadside shop from 1936. *New York Public Library*.

beaten path was definitely the way we traveled. We came upon a restaurant with its gravel parking filled with locals. If the joint was hopping with lots of action, we agreed this was a sure sign of great eats. We loved to sample fried chicken with a delicious taste and crispiness equal to my mother's home cooking. Once we settled down at a table near the window, my father eavesdropped to the jibber-jabber of nearby customers. It made him feel at home if he overheard someone speaking French, as that usually meant that there were Cajuns in the house. He would go over to shake hands. "You never know," he'd comment to us, "we may be cousins."

Sitting up tall, all prim and proper in a restaurant, we were thrilled to choose whichever dish we liked from the menu. Settling in for the grand experience, we began with a soda pop, which was quite a treat, as we had only Kool-Aid or well water to sip on at home. We ordered chocolate cake for dessert only if we had cleaned our plates. Leftovers were never taken home, as it was considered rude to walk out with an uneaten meal packed in a paper bag.

The doggie bag trend of leftovers was introduced during the 1940s, when Americans experienced shortages. Under President Franklin D. Roosevelt, limits were placed on the quantity of foodstuffs such as butter, coffee and sugar. Rationed items were expanded to include canned goods, red meat, dairy products and fats, which challenged many Americans to feed their families. If they also owned dogs, it made sense to take home leftover food, such as steak bones, from restaurant meals to feed their pets. Early doggie bags were printed with the sketching of a dog above the restaurant's name. Although there was a time when it was considered tacky to take home leftovers, the trend gradually expanded and became acceptable. This also discouraged diners from overeating large portions. It became sensible for Tuesday's dinner leftovers to be served as Wednesday's lunch by taking home the remaining uneaten entrée.

Our family adventures usually began on Memorial Day. Before the sun peeked above the horizon, our crew was already on the road to launch our trip. There was less traffic early in the day, and the temps were cooler. The girls were dressed in pajamas. We rubbed sleep from our eyes as we tumbled into the backseat of our baby-blue two-door Ford Fairlane. Suitcases, folding chairs, a hotplate for cooking and a picnic basket had been loaded in the trunk the night before. Because he didn't want to miss out on the best food in the South, my father asked for suggestions when we stopped at a roadside stand to buy a bushel of juicy peaches. "Where do you suggest we break for lunch up ahead?" he'd inquire.

If my father lucked into spotting a drive-in restaurant up ahead, he'd screech on the brakes while veering off the road to enjoy a homemade hamburger with fried onion rings for lunch. Carhops precariously skated over to our car as they balanced a tray piled on with drinks, hamburgers and malts. The curb service phenomena of serving fast food to customers in their cars began at drive-in restaurants in the 1920s, when the Pig Stand opened in Dallas, Texas. Carhops were both male and female, although during World War II, more women served as carhops as men joined the military. Their colorful uniforms, topped off with a sporty cap, became memorable symbols of the period.

My sisters and I took turns resting on the window ledge of the rear window, watching as trees and handwritten yard signs of "Farm Eggs for Sale" whizzed by. With excitement, we chanced upon a small town hosting a Fourth of July parade. Since my dad was not familiar with the one-way streets leading to who knows where, he took a chance by following a line of cars. Unbeknownst to us, the caravan was actually part of a Main Street parade, and we managed to be at the end of it. We pretended that we were VIPs as we waved to the crowd and rolled through the parade following snazzy convertibles, tractors pulling floats and marching bands. My only regret was that we didn't have a red-white-and-blue streamer as we joined the festivities.

Stuckey's began in the South during the Great Depression and remains popular for its pecan candies. *Courtesy of Stuckey's.*

"Don't you think it's time to stretch our legs?" my mother announced when she spotted a Stuckey's billboard sign up ahead. That was her way of saying that her sweet tooth was ready for fudge. With its homey atmosphere, Stuckey's was a magical, multipurpose place for us, serving as a store, restaurant, gas station, bathroom break and gift shop. My sisters and I had saved up dimes to buy a trinket from the scads of novelty items.

Stuckey's had a humble beginning during the Great Depression. Pecan farmer W.S. Stuckey Sr. owned a family orchard in Eastman, Georgia. In the early 1930s, with his pecans in tow, he built a roadside stand to attract drivers en route to Florida by displaying batches of his wife Ethyl's homemade pecan candy. After seeing early success during the 1940s, they sold their roadside stand and opened their first retail store in Georgia, soon adding two more in Florida. Their pecan treats became a symbol of a Southern delight, leading to further growth of Stuckey locations.

As we wandered through the countryside, we were whisked off to a town square in East Texas bordered by tidy neighborhoods. Across from the courthouse and next to the gazebo, a group of men wore John Deere caps and chewed on toothpicks as they enjoyed playing their daily checkers game. Once we lucked out on finding a good parking spot with the coins

Entertaining ice cream specialists were called soda jerks beginning in the 1920s. *Library of Congress.*

already in the meter, we headed to the five-and-dime store, then to the old-fashioned drugstore to order a milkshake. The soda jerk waved from behind the ice cream counter, where he poured root beers, scooped ice cream and made floats. These entertaining ice cream specialists became known as "soda jerks" because of the "jerking" motions the server used in swinging the soda fountain handle back and forth to make delicious treats. The pairing of drugstores with soda fountains gained popularity during the 1920s. Adding a soda fountain may have filled the void of socializing, which had declined during Prohibition when taverns shut their doors. Teenage boys became soda clerks and prepared creamy milkshakes made of milk, ice cream and flavorings.

Before dusk, we'd hunt for lodging with a swimming pool and would often find an Alamo Plaza Hotel Court to serve as our overnight retreat. This chain of Southwest adobe stucco–style buildings resembled San Antonio's Alamo. Started in Waco, Texas, in 1929, it was considered the first motel chain in the United States. We welcomed something roomy with two bedrooms and a kitchenette.

There's a song proclaiming, "The stars at night, are big and bright; deep in the heart of Texas." And Big "D" Dallas was a destination we enjoyed as we picked our favorite animals at the zoo and looked down from the top of the Ferris wheel at Six Flags. As my mother said, we also "spent time in Mexico" by enjoying dinner at the downtown El Fenix Restaurant,

Alamo Plaza. *Library of Congress*.

which was opened by the Martinez family in 1916. It was here that we were introduced to Mexican cuisine. My father surprised us when he spoke to the waiter in Spanish terms he had picked up along the way. It was our first time feasting on tamales—a blending of cornmeal, spicy shredded pork and green chilies. The refried beans were a perfect side dish, a change from the red beans and rice we were accustomed to at home. And how we enjoyed crunching what I called the "taco sandwiches." Our feast was topped off with sopapillas dipped in honey. Our waitress always received a nice tip, as my father recalled his gratitude at receiving a tip during his earlier lean years of delivering telegrams by bicycle as he worked his way through college.

A trip to north Louisiana coincided with the celebration of my mother's birthday in late July. We visited the Watermelon Festival in Farmerville to enjoy a parade and contests galore—watermelon eating, seed spitting, decorating, largest home-grown melons and a bout or two of arm wrestling. Although my family did not enter any of these competitions, we did enjoy slices of the juicy fruit.

Another memorable meal was at a luncheon eatery in a wood frame house. The wraparound porch was cooled by ceiling fans. With a breeze coming through after a quick rain and a blue sky with cotton candy clouds, we enjoyed the outdoors and picked a table under a magnolia tree. As we listened to the cooing of doves, we enjoyed fried catfish, purple hull peas and a sweet sampling of golden mayhaw jelly slathered on our Southern biscuits.

Our lunchtime also became a sobering history lesson when we learned that at one time, cafés such as this one did not allow African Americans to enter as customers. My dad had a way of telling a story that kept us mesmerized as he explained that during the late 1950s, Woolworth's was a popular five-and-dime chain store throughout America and its lunch counters were popular for quick bites. We recalled our frequent shopping trips to the Woolworth's in downtown Lafayette, where we enjoyed grilled cheese sandwiches and a slice of pie in the dining area.

Unexpectedly, Woolworth's became the focus of national attention in 1961, when four African American college students sat at the "whites only" lunch counter in Greensboro, North Carolina. They were hungry and attempted to order lunch, as did other diners. Though the young men were denied service because they were Black, they courageously refused to leave. The police were called in, and the situation led to news coverage as the story spread. This incident spurred more sit-ins throughout America.

In Louisiana, a similar sit-in occurred when seven students from Southern University in Baton Rouge sat down to order lunch at Kress, a popular downtown eatery. They were arrested for breaching the peace. Similar protests occurred for equal access to public accommodations until the Civil Rights Act of 1964, which outlawed racial segregation in public places, was passed under President Lyndon B. Johnson.

Our next stop was circled in red on our state map as we traveled through north Louisiana, venturing to where outlaw lovebirds Bonnie and Clyde were ambushed in 1934. Although we had missed seeing the pair's graves in their hometown of Dallas, we did view the historical marker near Arcadia, Louisiana, commemorating the site where the law ended the gangsters' crime spree. My dad filled us in about the duo's rip-roaring time through the South, where they robbed gas stations, small stores and banks. He also relayed the story that the partners in crime must have had a sweet tooth, as during their jaunts, they were known to have stopped at Lea's Pies in Lecompte, Louisiana, to sample a slice of the famous treats. Still a nostalgic setting, Lea's was always a target on my family's radar as a dessert break whenever we were in central Louisiana. Opened in 1928, originally as a garage, Lea's slogan proclaims, "Pie Fixes Everything."

One summer, we traveled to the Mississippi Gulf Coast to build sandcastles at the beach. Ever keen to share new cuisine and experiences with his family, my father suggested that we drive north just a little ways for some "Praise de Lard." I mistakenly guessed that we were heading to some sort of a religious revival. It wasn't what I expected at all.

As we bumped along a dusty back road, we could smell the scent of cooking a mile before we arrived. "Well kids, we've made it to heaven," my father announced as we stopped in front of a red falling-apart shack, topped with a handmade sign, "Praise de Lard BBQ." We jumped out of the car, finding our way to one of the rickety picnic tables. We were served our first taste of lightly tinged barbecue ribs. They oozed sweetness and spiciness at the same time. The pork and beans were abandoned as we switched our focus to the meaty delights. We couldn't seem to get enough as we gnawed away at juicy ribs, licked our fingers and scrambled to grab more. Without batting an eye, the pit master declared that our family looked as happy as "a tick on a pig." And I guess that was good, because we were happy as we guzzled down sweet tea and sopped up barbecue sauce with cornbread wedges.

While we indulged on this slap-up feast, my mother reminisced about her introduction to smoked ribs, which was during an earlier family boucherie. The country gathering involved much scrambling to collect tables and tools to set up outdoor cooking stations. It was one of her favorite times, which

Preparing to cook a rice and gravy dish. *Courtesy of Annette Huval.*

she enjoyed with her family as a special occasion. The local priest was always invited, and he blessed the event early in the day.

It was at one of these get-togethers that she and her sister collaborated on preparing the specialty of pig's stomach, called *ponce* in French. After the pig's stomach was meticulously cleaned out, it was stuffed with sausage meat. It was baked in a low oven similar to how a roast is cooked. Hours later, when the masterpiece was done, the cooks exclaimed how prettily the ponce had turned out. Surely it was the best that they had ever cooked, how delicious it would taste—everyone would enjoy it. You would have thought they were presenting a baby to the rest of the family with all the praise they shared in tribute to the cooked pig's stomach. All the ponce was missing was a baby bonnet! Such was the love for all of the wonderful pork dishes.

Our wanderlust treks through the South were precious. Stopping at one-of-a-kind joints was a pleasure. As my family and I rambled through big cities, along bayous and on Main Street USA, spanning our beautiful country, our many unplanned side trips led to unforgettable surprises. "What's the rush?" my father asked with an infectious smile. He never admitted that we might actually have been lost.

1

T-COCHON
(WE MEAN "LITTLE PIG")

I am fond of pigs. Dogs look up to us. Cats look down on us.
Pigs treat us as equals.
—Winston Churchill

When you grow up in Louisiana, chances are good that you have been led to a dinner table where a gamut of tasty bites are served on a platter—nutria stew, alligator kabobs, cow brain, baked possum, boiled crawfish or stewed blackbird. Well, you get the picture. The list of these one-of-a-kind dishes lovingly prepared by Southern cooks is endless. Don't you wonder what possessed a brave soul to be the first to sample a raw oyster by swallowing it whole or throw a cow tongue into a stew?

There comes a time when you become acclimated to finding a hog's head peeking up at you from Grandpa's outdoor chopping block. And this brings us to a passion for the Cajun pig, the source of countless Louisiana spreads—boudin, cracklings, pork chops, bacon or ham.

Many's the time when you have entered Grandma's kitchen and something wonderful is cooking under the lid of the black iron pot. It smells incredible, this mix of onions and meat. Grandma always proclaims it's chicken she's cooking, just to fool you into trying it, as you may not be keen to eat something exotic. You've learned to trust this little lady with her faded kitchen apron who reaches up to kiss your cheek as she slaps your hand with her wooden spoon when you try to get a sample of the dish. You've gone through this experience many times, knowing that the mystery meat is more likely to be a

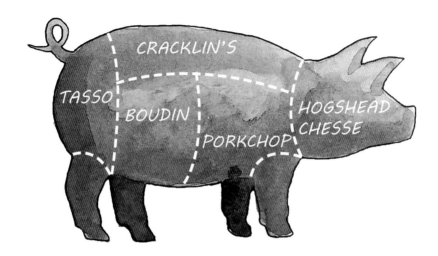

Many delicious dishes are derived from the Cajun pig. *Courtesy of Roby Poché.*

variety of animal parts like pig butt or cow tongue or some unpronounceable waterfowl. Even though Grandma doesn't use a measuring spoon and can't recite the recipe, she presents a tasty meal every time.

Le cochon has had quite a following of fans through the years; it was one of the first food animals to be domesticated. In some cultures, pigs are considered a symbol of wealth. According to the Chinese zodiac, people born during "pig years" such as 2019 may look forward to finding good fortune in their future.

Ironically, there are two St. Anthonys, and both are considered patron saints of swine. One hailed from Egypt and one from Padua, Italy. St. Anthony of Egypt is identified as the patron saint of not only swine but also swineherds. He is often depicted in paintings as a hermit with a pig at his side.

A popular tradition in Spain honors both saints. In the medieval village of La Alberca, famous for its ham, one lucky pig roams freely throughout the village for six months. It is well fed, sheltered and spoiled by the citizens. The pig is known as El Marrano de San Anton, or "the pig of St. Anthony." Blessed on July 13, the feast day of St. Anthony of Padua, the pig is temporarily protected and treated with TLC. It continues to run around the village and wears a bell strapped around its neck to alert drivers, who stop their vehicles on cobblestone streets to escort the pampered pig to safety.

Vintage illustration of piggy sitting by the fire. *New York Public Library*.

How quickly the situation changes. The honored guest, namely the pig, becomes a platter of pork chops and is served for dinner on January 17, the feast day of St. Anthony of Egypt. It became a customary act of kindness for the pig to be donated to the poorest family in the village. In modern times, however, the village auctions off the pig for charity. On the day following the festival, townspeople lead their animals to church for a blessing and pray for good health and fertility.

Amid the transition of wild boar roaming freely through the thick forests and swamplands of Europe and Asia to today's farm animal that squeals, the pig packed up its pen and enjoyed a boat ride to America in the early 1500s.

Spanish explorer Hernando de Soto was commissioned to find gold in the New World and establish a Spanish colony. Along the way, he conquered Peru. Moving on with an entourage of six hundred soldiers, ten ships, two hundred horses and thirteen pigs, he landed in Tampa, Florida, in 1539. Famous for his discovery of the Mississippi River, de Soto was also dubbed America's "Father of the American Pork Industry" for introducing the domestic pig to America.

As European colonies grew by establishing settlements in the new frontier of America, the production of pigs thrived as a means to provide settlers with fresh meat, salt pork, and other preserved pork dishes. De Soto's thirteen pigs kept busy by multiplying to a count of seven hundred within a few years. Perhaps the colonists considered housing their families a priority and did not always fence in their herd of pigs and cows. The hogs were natural scavengers. They ran freely through nearby forests and were often hard to gather and left behind as the colonists sought better areas to settle. As the number of hogs increased, the male hogs became aggressive and grew long tusks. They reproduced quickly and became a nuisance; the feral descendants of the original Spanish hogs were responsible for killing many cattle. Colonists, as well as Native Americans, recognized that the hogs were an easy target for sport hunting. The end result was a variety of pork dishes; it was soon determined to be a versatile and delicious meat.

American pioneers traveled westward by covered wagons called prairie schooners. These travelers formed wagon trains and shared the burden of toting along bags of corn seed and pairs of crated pigs to stock their farms for providing sustenance. Although cows and sheep were valued and gradually transported out west, pigs multiplied more quickly.

The heartwarming Little House on the Prairie book series by Laura Ingalls Wilder reveals hardships of pioneer life in America's frontier. The family lives off the land by growing vegetables and raising farm animals, including a fat pig that had been fed corn for weeks. As winter sets in, the Ingallses, led by Pa, kills the pig in a similar fashion to the Cajun boucherie as a means of filling the pantry with meat. Once the pig is killed, its bristles are scraped off and preparations are made to butcher the pig. The pig is hung from a tree to simplify cutting out parts to prepare a variety of meats, such as ham, spareribs and sausage. Parts of the pig, including the heart, liver, tongue and head, are set to boiling in a vat until tender to make hogshead cheese. The Ingalls children consider butchering time a special occasion and use the pig bladder as entertainment to make a balloon for tossing back and forth. They also consider the pig's tail a tasty treat; the girls spear it on a stick and

Pastoral sketch of farmland. *New York Public Library.*

Pigs were one of the first food animals to be domesticated. *Library of Congress.*

toast it over hot coals before sharing the sizzling meat. Cracklings were also prepared and often added to johnnycake as enhancement, similar to the Cajun way of adding crackling bits to cornbread. Ideally, the meat could be preserved and salted to feed families through cold winters.

Thousands of settlers bravely picked up stakes in their established communities to travel westward during the 1840s on the Oregon and California Trails. Once gold nuggets were discovered in California in 1848, the California gold rush enticed thousands of prospective miners to head to San Francisco.

Keeping families connected from one end of the country to the other became critical. The Pony Express was established in 1860 as a relay business to deliver mail and telegrams. Considered heroes, Pony Express riders crossed eight states at breakneck speed through difficult weather and dangerous conditions. Employing eighty delivery men of strong endurance, the Pony Express lasted only for eighteen months; the system was replaced by the Pacific Telegraph Line. The riders stopped at stations for overnight boarding, replacing horses, and getting nourishment. Their meals were nothing fancy and were often served in a bucket; they included cured meats, mostly bacon, dried fruits, flapjacks, beans and hard biscuits that could break your teeth.

Prior to the Civil War, Southerners recognized swine as an important food staple. Pigs were low maintenance; they ate just about everything. They were quick breeders and also provided a convenient food source—virtually every part of the pig could be used. Set loose in forests where they could root and eat freely, the pigs, which became wild, were caught when the food supply became low. Swine were usually found on plantations because they were easy to raise and feed. Several meals could be provided by hosting communal pig slaughters. This ritual led to what we now recognize as Southern barbecues. A plantation typically included a kitchen and smokehouse located a short distance from the main house. Sausage, bacon and a ham would hang before a slow-burning fire for hours in preparation for a feast. Enslaved people who worked on the plantations were often given the lesser cuts such as pigs' feet and intestines, and they improvised by preparing creative dishes for their families. One soul food fave, chitterlings, is prepared from the small intestines of pigs and is labor intensive. First, the intestines must be thoroughly cleaned inside and out; they are then simmered along with onions and vinegar in a big pot until tender for a couple of hours. Chitterlings can also be fried, but preparing this dish is not for the faint of heart, as the process is accompanied by

Farm setting from the 1930s. *Library of Congress.*

a distinctive, pungent smell. This dish may be described on restaurant menus as "Kentucky oysters" or "wrinkled steak."

With the state's proximity to the Gulf Coast, Louisiana residents have experienced numerous hurricanes. When the calendar shows the beginning of hurricane season approaching on May 15, those who live along the Gulf Coast stock up on bottled water, check their flashlights and batteries and compile a survival food kit. Hurricane warnings are serious business, and families prepare for temporary, camp-style living. Gas up your car, hunt for a deck of cards to play bouree, buy air mattresses to house extended family members and protect your windows by boarding them up. Keep your white rubber boots—what we call "Cajun Reeboks"—handy for trudging through muddy yards. In advance of the storm, it may be a good time to light the barbecue pit and cook whatever meats you have in the freezer in case the electricity goes out due to windy conditions. Many gumbos or stews simmer on the stove in preparation for the storm that's a-brewing in the Gulf.

IF YOU MENTION NAMES like Camille (1969), Betsy (1965) or Katrina and Rita (2005), memories bring shivers to the survivors of these Louisiana storms. It's always a good idea to stock up on staples that can be served at room temperature: crackers, peanut butter, Oreo cookies and more. One backup dish in the hurricane supply kit, Spam®, is meat in a can that has been the brunt of jokes. But this chopped pork and ham dish serves an ingenious purpose, as it can be eaten either straight out of the can or "fancied up."

Spam stands for "Shoulder of Pork and Ham." A Louisiana variation, Spam Hot & Spicy, adds Tabasco® pepper sauce. This little delight in a can has come a long way from its creation by George A. Hormel. He opened a slaughterhouse and meatpacking facility in 1891 in Austin, Minnesota. Later, when his son, Jay Hormel, took over the business, he revamped the product in 1937, launching it as the "Meat of Many Uses." Spam spread worldwide when it was added to the diet of soldiers during World War II. With Allied forces fighting to liberate Europe, Hormel Foods provided fifteen million cans of food to troops each week. Just pop open the tin to enjoy the canned product; it enjoys a long shelf life and does not require refrigeration. The potted meat grew in popularity on both the British and American home fronts since all "real" meats were included in food rationing programs and Spam was not, making it more readily available.

Since Louisiana's early days, pork has reigned supreme at pig roasts, believed to have been hosted by Native Americans, although they can also be traced to African, French, German and Spanish cultures. A wooden frame was built for smoking the meat over an open fire.

The group of people who eventually became known as Acadians or "Cajuns" spent difficult years finding a permanent home. In the early 1600s, they were transplanted from rural areas of western France and sailed to coastal Canada to establish a French colony called Acadia. It was here in what is now called Nova Scotia that they found freedom to follow their Catholic religion while prospering as farmers and fishermen.

Over one hundred years later, the Acadians were exiled from Canada for refusing to swear allegiance to the British Crown and its church. They faced tremendous hardship as families were separated through the massive

Southern hog killing. *New York Public Library*.

The brown pelican is Louisiana's state bird. *Courtesy of Annette Huval.*

deportation called Le Grande Derangement. Thousands relocated to southern Louisiana, where they adapted to a new life among the bayous, swamps and prairies. While the Cajuns thrived in their lush surroundings, they developed a unique lifestyle, including cuisine, intermingling distinctive influences from other cultures within Louisiana, namely Spanish, German, Italian, Creole, Native American, African and French. Ever resourceful, the Acadians used their ancestral recipes while also introducing the fruits of their new terrain. They grew crops on fertile land along the bayous, hunted, fished and gathered herbs. Although they welcomed fishing and embraced the riches of the Louisiana bayous, the main source for meat became the portly pig. Meals were adapted based on what was accessible to the Acadians. Once their pork-eating tastes were defined, they did not waste any part of the pig—all the way from the snout to the intestines to the piggy tail. Although the Acadians relished the riches of the sea and bayous, the versatility of the precious pig is why so much pork was consumed.

2

COCHON DE LAIT

ochon de lait is a French term for the special occasion of roasting a suckling milk-fed pig on an open hardwood firepit. In Louisiana, a cochon de lait also translates to a spirited social gathering filled with music, dancing and merriment.

Although Avoyelles Parish is in central Louisiana on a map, this rural parish has its heart farther south in Cajun Country through deep French roots. Established in 1860, the town of Mansura located in Avoyelles Parish was named by French general Napoleon Bonaparte's soldiers, who were early settlers. Comparing the Louisiana prairie land to the prairies of Egypt, near the Nile River, the soldiers tagged the town Mansura, which means "victorious" in Arabic.

In early days, the town prospered as a railroad hub and hosted a handful of cotton millionaires who ran cotton gins in the region. Mansura sat on high ground and was not prone to flooding, so it proved suitable as a tent city to house evacuees from nearby towns during the Great Flood of 1927.

The friendly community considered incorporating local customs through its centennial celebration in 1960. Town leaders of Mansura agreed to revive an old method of roasting a whole pig. In Mansura during the early days before refrigeration, boucheries and cochon de laits were a common way to share meat with neighbors. Since farmers grew swine, they were accustomed to building outdoor makeshift roasters for hanging a pig on a wire rack and cooking it over a stack of wood. Rather than baking a ham or turkey for holiday dinner, roasting a pig became customary in the rural parish. Farms

Above: Cochon de Lait. *Author's collection.*

Left: Swine on a farm. *New York Public Library.*

were plentiful, and all farm animals served a purpose. Chickens were raised to provide eggs, or they were cooked in a gumbo; cows were milked, and pigs were roasted.

Amid the toe-tapping sounds of musicians like Percy Sledge and Wayne Toups, there's usually a giant inflatable pig welcoming visitors to "Hog Heaven," where mouthwatering slow-cooked pork and all the fixings are sampled. A full slate of endless weekend entertainment at the Cochon de Lait festival is guaranteed through a parade, beauty pageant and other contests introduced at the celebration which continue today.

Ernest Juneau ran away with first prize for the boudin-eating contest in one of the early competitions. He was crowned "Boudin King" for eating six and a half pounds, equaling eight feet of boudin, within the allotted time.

Today, the contest rules have changed to ease the strain on the digestive system, with competitors eating three pounds of boudin within the shortest time span. Amazingly, the current seven-time champion reigns from Bangor, Maine, and became familiar with the popular Cajun delicacy of boudin through friends in Avoyelles Parish.

What a spectacle to behold when things go "hog wild" through a romping Greasy Pig Contest. Within a round pen ninety feet wide, a couple of greased pigs sized at thirty-five pounds trot out. Once they are turned loose, there's plenty of squealing going on—from the pigs as well as from the kids. Mud flies as oiled-up pigs cause chaos while trying to escape. A variety of age divisions in competition make the running of the pigs entertaining, although the kids' version has the biggest fan base. The kids have to not only catch the pig but also hold onto it and sack it. And the reward for all of the sweat and scampering is the perky pig, which is handed over to the winner.

What's the best way to call a pig to come over to you? Do you call him by name? Cry out "Soo-ey"? Or do you imitate the pig's grunting? The Mansura Cochon de Lait hosts hog calling contests for both adults and children.

The centennial celebration was so well received in 1960 that the town decided to keep the festival going annually and scheduled it during the second full weekend in May. Such a big event took a lot of effort through volunteers. In the early 1970s, the town's high school senior class cleared the street after the festival's Saturday night *fais do do* (street dance). In exchange for sweeping and hauling away a mountain of empty beer cans and food wrappers, the senior class was paid $250 to use toward graduation activities. The tidying up proved successful, as by 9:00 a.m. Mass at the downtown Catholic church on Sunday, everything had been cleared out and cleaned spic and span with no evidence of the previous night's celebration. High schoolers also participated in a goodwill tour to promote the festival to legislators in Baton Rouge, Lafayette and Opelousas.

The festival was once held in the downtown area, and cooks were enlisted to help roast the pigs, which averaged thirty pounds apiece. Originally, the small pigs were cooked on open fire. The head was chopped off and plopped into a large kettle of boiling water. Once the mishmash was tender, it was used to make hogshead cheese.

Through innovative engineering, the pigs are now cooked rotisserie style, roasting over an open fire overnight. In time, the festival spread out from the downtown area to a nearby festival site of fifteen acres, including a pavilion and paved parking lot. To accommodate the large number of

Left: Many opportunities for piggy events in Louisiana. *Author's collection*.

Right: Mansura Cochon de Lait is one of Louisiana's oldest festivals. *Courtesy of Mansura Cochon de Lait*.

pigs, a permanent cooking rack with a metal roof was constructed in front of the Dr. Jules Charles Desfossé House. As the oldest house in Avoyelles Parish, the 1790 Desfossé House belonged to Mansura's second mayor. Of French Colonial design, the home, now restored, features mud walls and wooden roof shingles.

For Cajun boucheries or pig slaughter, a fat pig is preferred over a leaner pig to prepare the pork dishes of cracklings, which are tastier with a bit of fat. However, when planning for a cochon de lait, a slimmer pig, called a "finishing pig," proves more desirable. Once the pork is sizzling and the skin is slightly crisp after sixteen hours of overnight cooking over oak and sweet pecan wood, chunks of the tender meat are pulled apart. When it's halfway done and the fat is dripping, the pig is flipped to ensure even cooking. When it's time to pig out, steamy morsels are served in plate lunches accompanied with rice dressing and a side of caramelized yams. In 2000, a record number of fifty-five butterflied pigs were hung vertically as the rotisserie spun slowly.

As festival attendance grew in the postage stamp–sized town, so did the unruliness, leading locals to compare the event to a small-scale Woodstock. To let things settle down, the event went on hiatus after the 1972 festival, which boasted the highest attendance of 100,000 visitors.

Gradually, the Mansura Chamber of Commerce was reactivated, and in 1987, through a community effort, the three-day porky party celebrating the culinary heritage of Avoyelles Parish returned to fund community improvement projects.

Cultures outside of Louisiana look at our festivals with a deep wonderment. The director of a Japanese film company heard of the magnitude of Mansura's Cochon de Lait. With a sense of curiosity, he wanted to sample and film a variety of America's celebrations. At the other end of the spectrum and across the country was a totally different type of festival than Mansura's celebration of the pig. The film crew began with the Tulip Festival in Seattle, Washington. Once everything had bloomed in Seattle and footage was in the can, the crew packed up their cameras to travel to Mansura to cover its foodway traditions by focusing on three families. One of them was the Bordelon family, headed by Nicky Bordelon, who has been involved in the Cochon de Lait for over forty years. Although the love of pork was an important part of the documentary, Bordelon enjoys hunting and opted to cook wild rabbit. His home kitchen was set up like a TV cooking show with all the ingredients and kitchen tools laid out. He prepped the rabbit on film as though he were appearing on the Food Network. And the film crew from Japan were amazed by the stories they had captured in such a unique setting.

The tradition of going hog wild by hosting a pig roast is practiced in other regions outside of Louisiana.

A pit is set up while a one-hundred-pound pig is slathered with a vinegary basting sauce. Puffs of smoke rise above the marshes of North Carolina, where an event called a Pig Pickin' celebrates the slow-cooked porcine delight. Ever since Sir Walter Raleigh brought the tobacco leaf to the New World from Europe, North Carolina farms have cultivated tobacco. As a way to celebrate successful tobacco harvests, farmers began hosting pig roasts. So popular were these events that the state has been declared "Pig Pickin' Capital of the World," referring to the deliciousness of falling-off-the-bone roasted pork. The traditions of these pig roasts also include serving Southern favorite side dishes such as coleslaw, hush puppies, baked beans, biscuits and sweet tea (well, maybe beer, too). This pulled pork event even has its own dessert—the Pig Pickin' Cake—which is usually brightened with mandarin oranges and crushed pineapple. South Carolina, considered the birthplace of barbecue, is also on the bandwagon of hosting celebrations with a pig pickin' event.

In many Latino households throughout the United States, the practice of a La Caja China pig roast is one way of honoring special occasions. Pronounced *ca-ha chee-na*, it's Spanish for "Chinese box."

Chef Martin Liz owns a catering venue and pop-up supper club called Lost Kitchen in Key West, Florida. Themed meals are hosted and highlight diverse cuisines such as Brazilian, Latin, Indian and New Orleans jazz brunches. These special events introduce a variety of cultural dishes and music to south Florida.

Years ago, the mountains of Cuba were carpeted with tobacco fields. Pig roasts commemorated Noche Buena (Christmas Eve), birthdays or weddings. A hole in the ground was dug and housed the cook pit. A whole pig was placed in the pit, and a fire was lit for the roasting. Many hours later, the roasted pig was served as a feast, accompanied by side dishes of black beans and rice.

As people moved closer to Havana for work opportunities, a caja china metal roasting box was designed to conform to the old traditions. Roasting a pig no longer meant spending time to dig a hole in the ground. Instead, a metal box two feet wide by one foot deep by four feet long is used. No holes are punched in the metal box, while the tin lid is topped with charcoal. To ensure even cooking on both sides of the pig, the box is opened up periodically and the pig flipped over.

Growing up in a farm setting in south Florida, complete with goats, chickens and pigs, Chef Martin was introduced to preparing meals by using the meats from animals that his family raised. They regularly hosted neighborhood pig slaughters. First, the pig was killed and bled, and the blood was saved to make blood marcillo sausage—no part of the pig is wasted. Pork skin is fried to make chicharron, a snack similar to Cajun cracklings.

In preparing for a caja china today, Chef Martin brines the pig for twenty-four hours using a mixture of salt, sugar, citrus, garlic, onions and other herbs. Rubbing the pig with butter and salt ensures a crispy skin during the cooking process. An extra touch of a mojo crillo marinade is used for meat tenderizing. The pig's ribs are filled with a sauce of sour orange, cumin, garlic, coriander seeds and oregano. After several hours of roasting, the outcome is moist, succulent meat with crackling, smoky skin.

3

CAJUN BOUCHERIE

Preparation for an autumn boucherie began soon after the first cold snap appeared over the levee in southwest Louisiana. Leading up to the communal pig slaughter, pigs were penned and fattened by increasing the amount of grain in their diets. This ensured muscular legs and a rounded rump. November was an ideal time to host a boucherie in the country, as cooler weather helped with keeping the meat fresh. Many households in rural areas of Louisiana did not have refrigeration until the 1960s or later. The boucherie was certainly not a lavish affair. Rather, it was recognized as a necessity for feeding large families and also served as a way to prepare for upcoming holiday feasts. This dawn-to-dusk event became one big party for family and friends to sing, dance, play, joke, chase one another and work together to serve a day-long meal.

A boucherie always began early in the day. The natural routine in a farmer's life was to rise at rooster's crowing to begin the numerous chores that it took to run a farm. Setup for the boucherie began before sunrise; the menfolk in the household arranged outdoor tables, boiled water in big pots and laid out their favorite tools—cleavers, knives, a mallet and tongs—to slaughter the pigs. Virtually every part of the pig, from the snout to the tail, was used to prepare a dish. There was little waste, which is likely what the saying "whole hog" derived from, because guests at the boucherie savored every single bit. A cauldron filled with hog lard was used to fry cracklings until the meaty bits popped; these were served as a pleasing appetizer before other pork dishes were ready for sampling.

Boucheries begin at the crack of dawn when the rooster crows. *Courtesy of Roby Poché.*

Many tools are used in preparation for a Cajun boucherie. *Courtesy of Annette Huval.*

Music, food and dance are a vital part of every Cajun event. Musician Luke Huval plays the fiddle. *Courtesy of Annette Huval.*

Throughout the day, the event may have involved a fair amount of beer guzzling with alternating swigs of local moonshine. Stories were shared, often in a mix of French and English within the same sentence. Part of the afternoon fun included someone pulling out an accordion or fiddle to play some tunes as entertainment. To keep the kids from running in and out of the house and slamming the screen door, their time was occupied with scurrying around the pecan trees and playing outdoor games until lunch was served.

Hosting a boucherie nurtured a sense of community. It drew together brothers and sisters, aunts and uncles, cousins who often served as playmates. It was a big undertaking. Assignments were doled out, whether setting up stations, picking up sticks to keep the fires going, chopping onions, serving dishes or measuring rice for making boudin. The tasks of killing and carving the hogs required skill that was carried down from father to son. Since a sizable group of attendees was slated to be fed, several pigs rather than one sole swine were led to slaughter. Before a pig was shot in the temple, one of the cooks, usually the family patriarch, led a prayer in thanksgiving to honor the pig for supplying food for the gathering—although, admittedly, it had no choice in the whole affair. Its

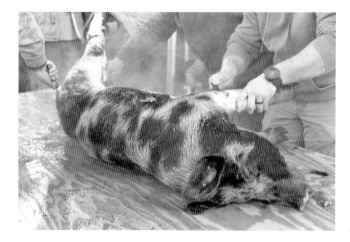

Scraping off the pig bristles. *Courtesy of Annette Huval.*

throat was slit through the jugular vein. It was hung by its feet and bled to make the actual slaughtering easier and cleaner. A bucket was used to capture the blood, which could be used to make blood boudin. Salt was added to the bowl of blood to prevent coagulation. The carcass was dunked into hot water to make the process of skimming off the hair by knife easier. Once cleaned, the carcass was laid on a table, and a saw was used to slice it down the breastbone. It was cut in half and continuously washed to remove blood and bone fragments. The backbone or back strap was cut away, as were other parts such as hams, which could be cured in sugar brine and smoked. Pork chops could be either cooked in a black iron skillet or baked in an oven.

As evidence of the swine's versatility, the organs of liver, heart, kidneys and stomach were harvested and used to prepare other specialty dishes such as debris or grillades. Cowboy stew is a popular way of slow cooking some of the organs in a camp-style fashion to prepare a hearty dish. The stomach lining is called *ponce* in French; this was rinsed out several times for a thorough cleaning to prepare for stuffing with sausage. Ponce is often cooked as a roast.

Pig intestines also served a purpose, as they could be used as casings to stuff andouille and boudin. The eyes, tongue, teeth, snout and ears were removed, as these parts were not usually used. The pig's head, however served a special purpose, as it is the key ingredient in making hogshead cheese. The head was removed and hung to allow for bleeding out, then boiled for hours along with the pig's feet. Vegetables such as onions and seasoning were added. Hogshead cheese is not actually a cheese at all. Rather, it is a jellied meat. The skin of the hog's head is ground and

Virtually every part of the pig from the snout to the tail is used to preparing a dish. *Courtesy of Annette Huval.*

mixed to prepare this delicacy with the consistency of pâté. It is usually transferred into a mold, and once cooled, it is sliced and may be served on crackers.

Meanwhile, it was common for the women of the household to work indoors and prepare boudin. This lighthearted task gave them the chance to work together as they shared the latest news about their family. They diced chunks of the pork meat to boil until tender. Onions, celery, bell peppers, green onions and garlic were chopped to add to the cooked meat, with seasoning sprinkled in. This was blended with cooked white rice. The mixture was inserted into a sausage casing, which was made from the pig's intestine. Often, a large cleaned-out horn of a bull was used as a funnel to easily guide the meat through to fill up the casing to make boudin links. Preparing sausage was a similar task, although no rice filler was used.

The piggy tail was removed and smoked to add a rich taste to a simmering pot of red beans later served over rice. Other cuts of meat were hung on hooks in the smokehouse to ensure great meals throughout wintertime. The pig's buttocks were salted to eventually produce ham. Other favorite cuts were shoulders and bellies. It was common to throw ham hocks or

Left: A boucherie is a Cajun communal pig slaughtering. *Courtesy of Annette Huval.*

Opposite: Jars of pickled beans, peaches and carrots. *New York Public Library.*

small chunks of smoked sausage into vegetable dishes such as butter beans, mustard greens or smothered potatoes to add protein. Many of these early side dishes that included pork tidbits have evolved into full-fledged entrées on today's dinner table.

Since families believed in using every part of the pig following a boucherie, an integral side product was lard, which served many purposes. The task of boiling the pig fat and rendering it into lard was just one more step of the boucherie. The lard could be used for frying cracklings. Bacon, derived from ribcage meat, could be preserved by being salt cured and stored in crocks in between layers of lard. Soap was also made by boiling lard in a cauldron along with lye or ashes collected from the fireplace. For scents, oftentimes rose petals, small bits of unused soap from the kitchen, lemon juice or perfume were tossed in. Once the soap had thickened, it was poured into molds such as chipped demitasse cups. After drying out for

a few days, the soap could be used for washing clothes on the washboard as well as for bathing.

To help with covering the costs of the boucherie, family members who did not own a pig but who participated shared fruits from their garden. Some homemakers spent hours searching their garden for green and red tomatoes, peppers and onions to prepare the Louisiana condiment chow-chow. This peck of pickled peppers in a jar is a much-loved relish. As a fixture on Southern tables, chow-chow adds spice to dishes, especially by adding a spoonful or two to gumbo or roast. In some places, it's called piccalilli.

An array of home treasures lovingly prepared by cooks included homemade bread and fig preserves to spread on the fresh slices. Pralines made from pecans picked earlier that season were shared at the family boucheries.

4

A VISIT TO THE CAJUN MEAT MARKET

Ike runs the country, and I turn the pork chops.
—Mamie Eisenhower

Before supermarkets stretched the length of a city block, many towns had smaller businesses dedicated to hardware, baked goods or fabric. The weary worn meat market wasn't like today's big-box stores. It was small, with room for twenty folks at the most if you counted the hunting dogs that customers brought in.

Strolling into an old-timey neighborhood meat market may transport you to earlier days when these one-stop shops were filled with various sundries. Some folks have ventured away from Cajun country and experienced a bout of homesickness for the nostalgia of squeezing a loaf of Evangeline Maid bread to gauge the freshness. Bags of Camellia brand dried red beans were stacked on the shelf alongside bright yellow Mello Joy Coffee cans and glass bottles of ground cayenne pepper. One row below were fly swatters and Duz laundry detergent promising the prize of a glass tumbler buried inside the powder. Shelves were packed with mouse traps or hairpins while more expensive items were placed at eye level for easy grabbing. Jars of pigs' feet floating in cloudy liquid lay on the shelf next to homemade wrapped pecan pralines. Kids raised a ruckus, asking for penny candy. Lively chank-a-chank music played on the radio while customers listened carefully to the musician's French twang.

General store from the 1930s. *Library of Congress.*

Your mouth waters in anticipation of enjoying some down-home cooking in the side kitchen of the country store. The menu includes entrées of smothered chicken or pork roast, and popular sides along with rice and gravy to fill up your plate lunch. Take in the aroma of what's cooking on the stove. The style of slow-cooking meat amid the Cajun trinity or mirepoix of onions, bell peppers and celery takes place in a black iron pot. There is jubilation from patrons ahead of you in eagerness of scooping up a mouthful of *bonne bouche*, French for "tasty bites."

On the counter is a giant rice cooker where fresh boudin links are curled and kept steaming hot. No matter in which Louisiana parish the shop resides, each spot enjoys its own distinct taste with a variation of texture, seasoning and chunkiness. Some have experimented with substituting white rice with cauliflower rice. A customer on the go may grab a box of saltine crackers along with a link or two of boudin. Visitors drop in for a cup of strong coffee, and they may add a drop of Tabasco hot sauce to their mug to perk it up.

As this little piggy goes to market, here are some popular Cajun pork preparations:

BACKBONE STEW is a dark and thick gravied pork dish—a favorite following a boucherie. The backbone (vertebrae) of the pig is cooked for hours.

BOUDIN is a savory combo derived from a variety of pig parts, including liver and intestines. Once the chopped-up boneless pork meat is cooked, seasoning, onions and cooked rice are mixed in. The wonderful blending is stuffed into a casing. In the old days, the actual pig's intestines could be used as the casing. Expert boudin makers have a sixth sense about ensuring that each link is uniform in size. Boudin resembles a sausage, though it includes the addition of seasonings and rice as filler. To further change the dish, you can squeeze the meat out of the casing, form it into a patty, pan fry on both sides and serve it with a fried egg on top. In many office settings, rather than a box of doughnuts displayed near the coffeepot as a treat for breakfast, you'll find boxes of boudin. Spirited discussions take place to determine which meat market produces the best boudin. Patiently, self-proclaimed carnivorous experts sample varieties to compare for color, amount of liver, ratio of meat versus rice portions and even ease in handling a link. Some have even developed their own grading scale for spiciness, mushiness and chunkiness. Louisiana cane syrup is often drizzled over the treasured snack. Variations of boudin have been created, as it can be smoked or fried as a "boudin ball" similar to a meatball.

Dishes of Cajun country have been far-reaching, including the almighty boudin. According to a journal written by frontier explorer Captain Meriwether Lewis, his crew sampled boudin blanc or white pudding prepared from a buffalo that he had hunted.

One of the many treasured Cajun delights—boudin. *Courtesy of St. Landry Parish Tourist Commission.*

Explorers Meriwether Lewis and William Clark were commissioned in 1804 by President Thomas Jefferson to lead an expedition across the United States. Their trek began in Illinois and ended in Oregon, and they were accompanied by a group of thirty-one others. Before President Jefferson signed on the dotted line for the U.S. acquisition of the Louisiana Purchase, he sought to find a direct water route to the Pacific Ocean for future trade.

Buffalo boudin was prepared during the Lewis and Clark expedition. *New York Public Library*.

Traveling on foot and by water, the adventurous entourage was introduced to a vast wilderness and new cultures, cuisine and plant and animal life during their treacherous trip. It was during these years that they discovered animals they had previously never encountered such as pelicans, beavers and buffalo. Their observations were noted in an elk skin–bound journal.

During Lewis and Clark's time in North Dakota, French Canadian fur trapper Toussaint Charbonneau and his Native American wife, Sacagawea, joined the expedition. The couple had many talents and proved valuable to the journey, as they were familiar with the lay of the land that they traveled. They spoke many languages, which was useful when they approached other cultures, and they also proved handy with campfire cooking. While camping out in Montana, Charbonneau prepared boudin blanc, a sausage made from a meat and kidney mixture they stuffed in a casing of buffalo intestines, then twisted and tied it into a link similar to today's boudin. Boiled and lightly fried in bear grease by Charbonneau, the boudin was declared a delicacy.

CHAURICE (shore-eez) is fresh and spicy pork sausage used to enrich gumbo, jambalaya and red beans and rice. It evolved from Spain's chorizo.

CHITTERLINGS are sometimes called the "trash" of the pig or intestines and may stink to high heaven while simmering on the stove, but the result is deemed gratifying. Often paired with mustard greens, this dish may also be eaten boiled, breaded or fried.

CRACKLINGS, CRACKLINS or GRATONS. Fans saunter out of the meat market with brown paper bags full of the crunchy tidbits of pork skin and fat. Once the cracklings are fried twice in big, open kettles, there's a generous sprinkling of cayenne pepper. Generally, these morsels are made from either pork skin or pork belly and fried until crispy. They turn golden brown on the outside and are tender inside, like a pork French fry. Adding crackling bits to a cornbread batter is popular.

You can't eat just one crackling! *Courtesy of St. Landry Parish Tourist Commission.*

DIRTY RICE, also known as rice dressing, is a mix of ground pork, chicken livers and gizzards and cooked rice. It's considered a side dish, though it contains meat. However, diners also enjoy packing a hollowed-out bell pepper with rice dressing and topping it with seasoned breadcrumbs. The stuffed red, green, orange or yellow bell peppers are baked for forty minutes, and this versatile main dish is ready for sharing.

ETOUFFEE (a-too-fay) is a French cooking term meaning "smothered within a covered pot." Served at the kitchen table are varieties of etouffee that include chicken, potatoes and sausage or the famous Breaux Bridge Crawfish Etouffee.

FRICASSEE (free-kay-say) is a thick, chunky stew prepared by browning and then removing the meat of choice from the pan. A roux is made from pan drippings and then the meat is returned to the pan for slow cooking in the luxurious gravy known as a fricassee. Chicken fricassee is a timeless dish served from a cast-iron pot.

GRILLADES (gree-yahds) are also called debris or routee. They are cuts of beef or pork marinated in spices and herbs for grilling or slow cooking. Grillades and grits is a popular Southern dish suitable for brunch.

Above: Pig organs used to cook debris. *Courtesy of Annette Huval.*

Left: Smoked sausage with jalapeño pepper. *Courtesy of St. Landry Parish Tourist Commission.*

GUMBO is a thick soup cooked for hours using seafood or meat, countless spices and vegetables like onions, bell peppers and celery. It is served over rice. A successful gumbo begins with a roux, which can be used as a thickening agent and also adds a deeper color to the dish. There are variations of gumbo—shrimp and okra, duck and andouille, seafood with crabmeat and shrimp and chicken and sausage gumbo in which a chunk of tasso is added for a richer taste. To add extra protein to a gumbo, some cooks drop in a peeled hardboiled egg. Sweet potatoes baked in their skin can complete this simple meal as a side dish. It may seem like an acquired taste, but many locals enjoy placing a scoop of potato salad in the middle of the gumbo. The word *gumbo*, or *gombo*, is an African term for "okra." One of the most infamous gumbo recipes ever shared was when Disney promoted its 2009 animated fairy tale *The Princess and the Frog*, set in Louisiana. A recipe was launched for "Princess Tiana's Healthy Gumbo," which used quinoa instead of rice. Other suggested ingredients in the recipe included kale, stewed tomatoes and whole wheat flour instead of traditional roux. The dreary gumbo lacked the Cajun touch of spices, drawing an outcry from Louisiana foodies who saw little similarity between an authentic Cajun gumbo and Princess Tiana's dish.

HOGSHEAD CHEESE is a Cajun pork pâté that really isn't cheese but rather a meat jelly. A variety of pig parts, such as the head and pig's feet, are boiled for hours to prepare this jellied meat, which can be sliced and served on crackers. In some Southern states, it is called souse.

JAMBALAYA is a one-pot dish that includes meat and/or seafood and rice. A good place to begin in preparing this hearty meal is by checking for leftovers in the fridge. Cooks throw in a variety of andouille, chicken, beef, ham, pork bits or shrimp along with vegetables, spices and rice. A derivative of jambalaya, *ya-ya* is an African word for rice.

PONCE is the stomach of a pig stuffed with sausage meat. Also known as gog, hog maw or chaudin, it resembles a roast and may be cooked in an oven or smoker.

RED BEANS AND SAUSAGE AND RICE is a main dish prepared with dried kidney beans that are soaked in water overnight and served over a bed of rice. Usually made with chunks of andouille, sausage or tasso, this comfort food dish was traditionally served on Mondays, which was considered washday in big families. Red beans and rice is an easy dish to have simmering on the stove, requiring little prep work and tending to, allowing the housekeeper to take care of the other duties of running a household.

ROUX (roo) is crucial as the root of many rustic Cajun dishes as a thickening agent for gumbo, fricassee and etouffee. *To thine own self be true, when making a gumbo, start with a roux!* To save time, some cooks purchase one of a variety of brands of jarred roux or dry powdered roux. The roux may be dark or light in color, depending on preference. Many cooks compare the ideal color of the roux to the color of a brown paper bag, while some prefer the richer hue of chocolate. Ingredients of a roux are usually equal parts of butter and flour or equal parts of cooking oil or hog lard and flour. Using hog lard makes the dish especially full-bodied. This tradition stems from the time when families hosted boucheries and used virtually every part of the pig, including the fat. A successful roux is cooked slowly in a pot and may prove to be a good exercise in building your arm muscles by continuously stirring with a wooden spoon.

Sauce Piquante is a spicy sauce with a tomato base. Just about any meat such as chicken or seafood can be used to cook this dish, although turtle meat is especially popular. Get ready to dig into slow-cooked red sauce served over rice.

Tasso is a smoked Cajun ham made from the pork shoulder and cured in a salt box. It may be smoked and heavily spiced. Once the ham is chopped in smaller pieces, the smoky taste is a good addition to gumbos and mustard greens.

5

PORK PARTIES

The love of pork is celebrated through a quirky array of festivals and cook-offs. There's something smokin' hot about each, with the common themes and elements of music, arts and crafts and a grab bag of exceptional food.

ACADIANA BACON AND BOUDIN COOK-OFF

(Lafayette)

Novices and seasoned aficionados alike are drawn to this October fete in downtown Lafayette to sample and vote for the top-rated boudin. Boudin eating contestants are cheered on as live music plays and dancers are in the throes of zydeco side-stepping. Miles of boudin links are lined up for sampling as attendees stroll from booth to booth to grab the meat and rice delicacy from vendors throughout the state vying for the title of the best boudin. Boudin specialties are reminiscent of a Forrest Gump bevy of dishes of pork rather than the movie's humorous list of shrimp, such as a pork belly and boudin ball slider with garlic/green onion aioli, boudin kolache with pepper jelly and pepper jack cheese, boudin eggroll, pecan-smoked boudin, crawfish boudin, venison and pork smoked boudin, boudin and fig pie, and boudin-apple with sweet and sour sauce. Our cooks are not afraid

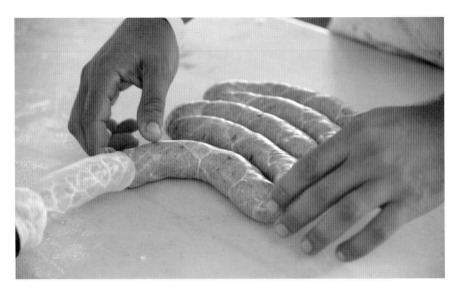

Preparing boudin during a boucherie. *Courtesy of Annette Huval.*

to borrow from other cultures, and that's how boudin lasagna was created. Another dish is the boudin king cake, which takes the Mardi Gras icon a few steps higher. This savory creation starts with bread dough that is stuffed with boudin, braided with two ends joined to form a circle and topped with crispy cracklings. Once baked, it is drizzled with Steen's pure cane syrup.

ACADIANA POBOY FESTIVAL

(LAFAYETTE)

Originating in New Orleans, the lusty poboy is similar to a submarine sandwich. But in the Bayou State, the bread used is traditionally a crusty French bread that gives a little crunch when you bite in. In the early 1920s, brothers Bennie and Clovis Martin worked as streetcar conductors with dreams of opening a restaurant in the French Market of New Orleans. Due to ongoing labor disputes in 1929, a group of streetcar workers who were also friends of the Martins began a transit strike. To lend support to their former colleagues, the crafty brothers patched together foot-long sandwiches. Crammed with a choice of cheese, meats or seafood and dressed with lettuce, tomatoes and mayo, those famous sandwiches were handed out freely to those "poor boys" on strike. Taste buds are on high alert when devouring and voting on the best poboys prepared by local shops at the Acadiana PoBoy Festival held on the first Saturday in April in downtown Lafayette. Platters are filled with specialties such as the Porchetta PoBoy and Chipotle Pork Carnitas. A "Boudin Pizza Burger PoBoy" made a grand entrance at this foodie festival. It's a one-of-a-kind combo with a boudin patty atop a burger patty slapped between two bun-like pizzas.

BALLOONS AND BOUCHERIE FESTIVAL

(GONZALES)

A boucherie festival was held every fall in Ascension Parish in the town of Sorrento, originally known as Conway though renamed in 1909 by German immigrant and developer William Edenborn. He named the town Sorrento to honor the city in Italy where he and his bride honeymooned. The town grew when opportunity for the lumber industry expanded. A railroad was built through this area, which was formerly covered with pine, sweet

Slow cooking in a black iron pot. *Courtesy of Annette Huval.*

gum, cypress and live oak trees. As more people settled in Sorrento, a fall boucherie was hosted to provide meals for families. At the end of a day of cooking, visiting, playing music and eating, each family received a portion of the butchered hog as their share of the day's work. To keep community spirit flourishing, the Sorrento Lions Club members began hosting a communal boucherie during the 1960s, and gradually the gathering was opened to everyone. The country autumn festival now combines the Ascension Hot Air Balloon as well as the Boucherie Festival and is held in nearby Gonzales. Boucherie activities include crackling and jambalaya cook-offs, a custom car show, pig roasts, a maritime rope-throwing competition, and now the added entertainment of hot air balloons glowing at night. The event is the prime fundraiser for the Louisiana Lions Eye Foundation and the Louisiana Lions Children's Camp.

BLACK POT FESTIVAL AND COOK-OFF AND BLACKPOT CAMP

(Lafayette and Eunice)

When setting up your kitchen tools in preparation for cooking up a storm of comfort food like gumbo, a cast-iron pot should be high on the list. Initial steps for "seasoning" the heavy pot are washing it in soapy water, drying it thoroughly, rubbing it lightly with vegetable oil and baking the pot in a hot oven for an hour. The new festival, which showcases dishes cooked in a black pot, is held at folklife park Vermilionville. It's a celebration of food, music, dance and camping. Cooking competitions are held in three categories: gravy (also includes etouffees and dishes like smothered pork chops), cracklings and jambalaya. On a cool October night, the setting is tranquil as the campfire crackles and dishes are slow cooked on giant black iron pots. The fiddler entertains with old-time French songs as everyone looks forward to a taste of gumbo. There's a slew of jumpin' and jivin' musicians like the Revelers, Pine Leaf Boys, swamp pop king Warren Storm, Yvette Landry, Sonny Landreth and Eric Adcock on the lineup. Proceeds go to benefit Louisiana Folk Roots.

The Black Pot Camp, a separate event but held in conjunction with the festival, takes place at the Lakeview Park & Beach in Eunice. Activities include performances by award-winning musicians from across the United States. Campers try their hand at learning how to play the Cajun fiddle, accordion,

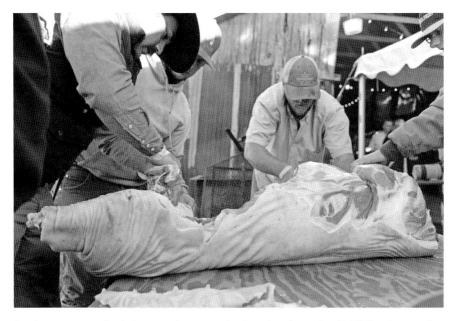

Southerners recognized pigs as an important food staple prior to the Civil War. *Courtesy of Annette Huval.*

guitar and banjo or take a stab at writing a song. Cooking demonstrations are also given.

Joseph Vidrine, a talented virtuoso of photography, cooking and performing music, embraces participating in events such as the Black Pot Camp to promote the Cajun culture. With a rich cultural background and fluent in French, as are both of his parents, Joseph is well versed in playing the accordion, banjo and fiddle.

Family boucheries were a way of life when Joseph was a young boy. Admittedly, he was fascinated with each step of a boucherie from facing the pig's snout to studying the process of butchering a pig to glean various cuts of pork. He looked forward to this event every winter and assisted with several boucheries as an adult, including performing one in Alaska, where pigs are rare. Grass-roots enthusiasts such as Vidrine have fostered a revival of boucheries. With carving tools in hand, Vidrine showed off his meticulous skill at preparing boudin and other favorite Cajun dishes. Curious onlookers were intrigued as Vidrine explained the Cajun tradition. As a hands-on promoter of his Cajun heritage, Joseph travels around the country to attend folklife festivals similar to Black Pot, where he shares the secrets of Cajun cooking and music. "Freelance Cajun" is what he calls himself, along with a blog and website (www.freelancecajun.com). By organizing Cajun jam sessions, preparing Cajun meals and demonstrating components of the native Cajun lifestyle, Joseph gives a glimpse into the alluring culture of southwest Louisiana.

After a full day of conducting music and dancing workshops through the "Adult Band Camp" of the Black Pot Camp, Joseph Vidrine and others scoot over to the barn, where the evening ends with a *bal de maison* (community dancing social) just like in the old days.

BON MANGE FESTIVAL

(GHEENS)

This community in Lafourche Parish was originally known as Vacherie, French for "cattle ranch." In 1879, cattle and sugar baron John R. Gheens of Kentucky purchased the property, expanding the ranch. A town named Vacherie in St. James Parish already existed, so the name Gheens was chosen in honor of the large landowner. Bon Mange ("good eating" in French) is a forty-plus-year festival that includes live music, auctions and a variety of Cajun dishes. One of the more popular is the grillades poboys. Grillades, also called debris or routee, are usually lesser cuts of pork shoulder or pork fingers. Once lightly pan fried, the meat is slow cooked in spicy gravy. Grillades may also be served over Southern grits.

Crawfish boudin and fried boudin balls. *Courtesy of St. Landry Parish Tourist Commission.*

BOUDIN FESTIVAL

(Scott)

It's held every April in the town of Scott, "Boudin Capital of the World." We celebrate the versatility of the popular rice and ground pork sausage we call boudin by enjoying it morning, noon and night. The focus on a variety of musical genres lends an opportunity for practicing Cajun jig dance steps. Aside from a boudin eating contest, there are also zydeco and Cajun dance competitions, arts and crafts and fireworks on opening night. The "Bou Crew," a group of former Boudin Festival Queens, assists with festival activities. For over seven years, the town of Scott, rich in Cajun heritage, has celebrated the mighty Cajun sausage.

CADIEN TOUJOURS BOUCHERIE

(Mermentau Cove)

A cultural loss was affecting the small community of Mermentau Cove, once considered a smuggler's refuge because of its strategic location near the Old Spanish Trail. Important parts of the much-loved Cajun way of life were trickling away. In an impassioned effort to preserve French Acadian customs, a nonprofit organization, Cadien Toujours (French for "Always Cajun"), was formed with ambitious goals of advancing the Cajun joie de vivre.

Its inaugural event was the tradition of a Courir de Mardi Gras, a "run" conducted by men who perform as runners bedecked in colorful, tattered clothing. They rode on horseback led by Le Capitaine. Others crammed into wagons as the caravan of merriment rolled down the back roads. Their lighthearted quest was to collect ingredients for making a communal gumbo. Through this run, a younger generation was introduced to participate in a spirited event in which their fathers or grandfathers may once have similarly entertained neighbors in exchange for a bag of rice or other produce.

One of the organizers of Cadien Toujours is Chance Henry, Acadia Parish native, who researched the origin of Courir de Mardi Gras to understand how many of the Cajun traditions of Mardi Gras are tied to a Catholic feast of medieval times. Chance had enjoyed his experiences as a Mardi Gras runner in the region but was encouraged to spearhead an effort to form a

Smoked sausages hanging. *Courtesy of Annette Huval.*

community group. He serves as Le Capitaine, who wears a long purple cape as he leads on horseback, followed by a wagon full of runners who wear scary homemade masks and tall pointed hats called capuchons. For the thrill of the chase of a chicken, they sing and perform wild antics such as rolling around in ditches or climbing trees, all for fun. The purpose of wearing a disguise for the runners stems from older days when men may have been embarrassed to be seen begging in the community for chickens, rice and sausage, which are the core ingredients for making a gumbo.

The momentum of the organization quickly spiraled upward when they agreed to spearhead another popular Cajun tradition. They organized a wintertime boucherie in which two pigs are killed: one for a cochon de lait (pig roast) and a heftier one for a boucherie.

The day's event has a fascinating lineup. It begins with a Catholic priest arriving at 6:30 a.m. to bless the event. He promises to return to the boucherie later in the day to enjoy a bowl of gumbo and tap his toes to the accordion music during the jam session.

Children aged eight to sixteen are invited to gather to perform a special task. It's understood that they should be familiar with using a rifle with supervision and also have an interest in being the chosen one to kill the pig for everyone to feast on. Many are accustomed to seeing family members

The child who draws the highest card will shoot the pig for the boucherie. *Courtesy of Annette Huval.*

pack up a gun and other supplies to head out to a hunt. A leader spreads a deck of playing cards, and each child selects a card. The one who pulls the highest card earns the privilege of shooting the pig for the boucherie.

The black-bristled pig is placed in a trailer pen, and its forehead is marked with an X. A blond-haired girl, aged ten, is thrilled that she has grabbed an ace out of the deck and is honored for the upcoming task. She's given directions on shooting the pig between the eyes at the marked X and is supervised as she aims and hits the pig on the first shot. The pig jerks a bit while the boucherie crew slits the animal's throat to begin the grisly bleeding process. A drop of blood is smeared on each cheek of young blondie as an initiation ritual, similar to when someone kills his or her first deer on a hunt.

The pig slaughter process takes nearly three hours, as several hands work together to drag the pig out of the trailer, bleed it and place it on a table to cut up the carcass. Some of the crew swish down a can or two of beer, as the day will be long with hard work ahead. An old-fashioned six-inch wooden tool with a metal disc called a hog scraper, purchased at a nearby flea market, is used to scrape off the pig's bristles. It's important to scrape off the bristles, as this will make the pig skin more appetizing during preparation of various dishes.

Simultaneously, a crew member pours scalding water to keep the pig and work area clean. At one end of the table, someone is slicing off the pig's head and impaling it on a post. During an old-fashioned boucherie, however, the pig's head and other parts are set aside, boiled and used to make hogshead cheese. At the other end of the butchering table, the pig's feet are cut off and may be used to prepare another dish. The carcass is sliced open, and the innards, such as the liver, kidneys and heart, are scooped out, placed in a metal bowl and scooted off to another crew member who will cook this as a debris rice and gravy. He's cooked dishes like this before. The smell of liver cooking is pungent as the meats slow cook.

Onlookers of all ages surround the butcher table to study the process as the pig is skinned. A reciprocating saw is used with ease to cut through bones and divide the ribs. The variety of cuts are well pronounced, and the young men are proficient in butchering the pig. The pig's tongue is cut out and tied to a string, which blondie twirls around. The pig was bled once its throat was slit, so there is not much blood remaining on the table.

The Cadien Toujours Boucherie is a ticketed cultural event. Admission is ten dollars for adults and includes filling meals of gumbo, boudin, jambalaya and more. Beer is available for sale. Rice cookers are full of fluffy grain; servers drop a scoopful in plastic gumbo bowls and add either gumbo, pork

A pig is the guest of honor at a Cajun boucherie. *Courtesy of Annette Huval.*

Crew members of the Cadien Toujours organization slaughter a pig for the communal boucherie. *Courtesy of Annette Huval.*

Left: Many dishes are prepared at a Cajun boucherie, usually held in the wintertime. *Courtesy of Annette Huval.*

Below: Music, socializing and an endless array of dishes at a Cajun boucherie. *Courtesy of Annette Huval.*

Above: Ham bone and red beans. *Courtesy of Camellia Beans.*

Left: Celebrate Mardi Gras with the Krewe of Red Beans. *Courtesy of Camellia Beans.*

Throw me something mister at the Red Beans Mardi Gras Parade in New Orleans. *Courtesy of Camellia Beans.*

Top: Red beans and rice is Monday's lunchtime staple. *Courtesy of Camellia Beans.*

Middle: Roasted pigs. *Courtesy of City Pork.*

Left: Boudin bits. *St. Landry Parish Tourist Commission.*

Hot boudin and plate lunches in downtown Lafayette at third-generation Johnson's Boucaniere. *Courtesy of Johnson's Boucaniere.*

During a boucherie, the pig bristles are scraped off at the Fete des Bouchers. *Courtesy of Chef John Folse.*

Many southwest Louisiana festivals fry cracklings. *Courtesy of Annette Huval.*

After killing a pig during a boucherie, it is dragged to a table for slaughtering. *Courtesy of Annette Huval.*

Comfort food of ham and beans. *Courtesy of Camellia Beans.*

During a boucherie, virtually every part of the pig can be used to prepare a delicious meal. *Courtesy of Annette Huval.*

Left: Cracklings are like pork "French fries." *Courtesy of Annette Huval.*

Below: Sprinkling Cajun seasoning on cracklings. *Courtesy of Annette Huval.*

Pig stomach, called *ponce*, cooking in a black iron pot. *Courtesy of Annette Huval.*

Sausage ready for the smokehouse. *Courtesy of Annette Huval.*

Cadien Toujours of Mermentau Cove promotes Cajun traditions. *Courtesy of Annette Huval.*

Suckling pig set up for roasting. *Courtesy of Annette Huval.*

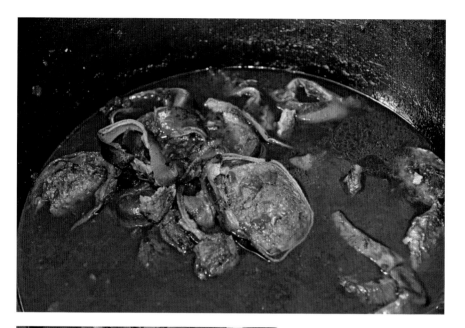

Above: Black iron pots are a vital vessel for slow-cooked Cajun dishes. *Courtesy of Annette Huval.*

Left: Delectable roasted pig. *Lost Kitchen Supper of Key West, Florida.*

Above: Butter beans with ham hocks. *Courtesy of Camellia Beans.*

Right: A cochon de lait. *Author's collection.*

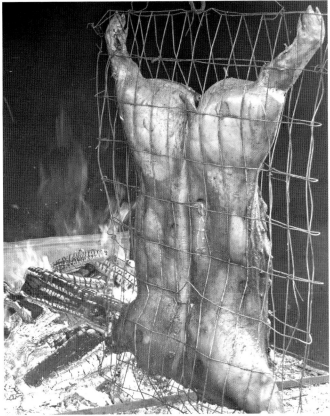

Above: You'll find crackling in Cajun meat markets. *Courtesy of St. Landry Parish Tourist Commission.*

Left: The thrill of the chase at the Courir de Mardi Gras in Church Point. *Author's collection.*

Cutting up the pig at a Cajun boucherie. *Courtesy of Annette Huval.*

Pulled pork sandwich. *Courtesy of National Pork Board.*

Pork and veggie kabobs. *Courtesy of National Pork Board.*

Smokin' hot sausage links. *Courtesy of Cajun Bayou Food Trail.*

Roasted pig. *Courtesy of Chef John Folse.*

Rice plays an integral role in many Cajun dishes. *Courtesy of Falcon Rice.*

Cochon de Lait row of pigs roasting. *Author's collection.*

Southwest Louisiana hosts many crackling cook-offs. *Courtesy of Annette Huval.*

backbone stew or debris rice and gravy with high praise from the guests. Sample-sized bits of smoked sausage are passed around, as are cracklings. Chaudin (stuffed pig stomach) and corn macque choux with tasso are cooked in large vats. Slices of hogshead cheese are served at room temperature as appetizers. One of the neighbors baked fig muffins, which are gobbled up quickly. Some of the meaty dishes take a few hours for slow cooking and may be infused with dark Cajun roux. Cooks at each station welcome questions about their techniques and the amount of seasoning sprinkled on the dishes.

The boucherie is held on the Henry farm. As a working farm in a rural setting, the farm is called Beau Chenes, which means "beautiful oaks." There are heads of cattle and a few donkeys roaming and rice fields that become crawfish fields in the right harvesting time. The Henrys have three generations that have participated in boucheries and are experienced in dividing the work. Within some families, rather than shooting the pig, a noose was made to hang the pig. Once its throat was slit, the pig was bled and blood was collected to make blood boudin, called blood pudding in some cultures.

Many of the boucherie activities, such as the cooking stations, jam session, bandstand and dance floor, are held in the Henrys' one-hundred-year-old barn, always lit up and ready for a party. The open barn is decorated with signage of sponsors of the boucherie while the Acadian flag, modified in the shape of a pig, hangs on the back slats of the barn.

The Henrys are encouraged by efforts ensuring that the French language and Cajun culture do not fade away. By hosting events such as the boucherie and the Courir de Mardi Gras, traditions will be passed on to younger generations. Cadien Toujours is a nonprofit organization that donates French books to area schools, supports French tables in which French speakers regularly meet for a social and sponsors Cajun dance lessons. There was a time when Louisiana children were punished for speaking French in the classroom. They received a quick tap on their fingers with a wooden ruler by *la maitresse* (schoolteacher). This earlier generation was discouraged from conversing about daily activities, and when they grew up and bore their own children, they often did not pass on the French language.

Every year, the boucherie grows in attendance. Goings-on fill up the day at the boucherie. With the beauty of sunshine covering the countryside, children mount a yellow buggy pulled by a tractor and are taken on a ride around the farm. There are no strangers here. Joining the jam session are a couple of accordion players, guitarist, fiddlers and a gentleman with a white cowboy hat playing a set of handmade spoons as a musical instrument.

Originally from Maine, by way of Canada, he grew up speaking French and is a recent transplant to Louisiana because of work opportunities. He fit right into the music session, and by the end, he was proclaimed a long-lost cousin.

The second pig was shot and bled the previous evening, and its head was also removed Saturday morning at dawn. It was prepared and butterflied to be placed between two metal grills that rotate for consistent roasting for six hours. It started out pale in color, and by late afternoon, the skin was bronzed and the smell was heavenly. The butchering table serves a second purpose and is thoroughly sanitized before it is used to prop the second pig, this one that was roasted. The roasted pork meat is tender and slightly charred as the boucherie team pulls it off the bone. Some wear gloves while others don't, maybe sampling a small chunk now and then. They joke that they are testing the taste of the meat before the others get hold of it.

There are subtle signs that this region also serves as cowboy territory as an elder begins a bullwhip demonstration. A collection of colorful plaited leather bullwhips is proudly displayed. The sharp sound of the whip is heard as two men, one young and one older, snap it sharply with a practiced turn of the wrist. On the range, the whip is cracked to control livestock.

Guests gather as the Cajun band begins to play a variety of tunes. Women often dance together on the makeshift dance floor, which has flour sprinkled on it to accommodate the fast-paced Cajun jitterbug dancers. Some dancing partners wear rubber boots and glide through a waltz. A dog searches for a bit of sausage that someone may have dropped as he rambles through the maze of partners on the dance floor. All enjoy the wailing of the Cajun song "La porte d'en arriere." The boucherie team has cleaned up nicely by removing their bloody aprons and pulled off their rubber boots to switch to cowboy boots. They are proud to wear shiny silver belt buckles and join in with the socializing of the event.

The blood-and-guts celebration of a boucherie represents much more than slaughtering a hog or two. It brings back a time-honored way of life. The challenges of the Cajun Nation have included picking up roots in France and settling in Canada, only to be banished from Canada to search for a new home in a new land. We've experienced hurricanes, have lost much of our Louisiana coastline and are often been misunderstood because of unfavorable representations in movies. Of course, we also cringe when we travel out of state and peruse the menu of an "authentic" Cajun café that serves gumbo with tomatoes in it. We have wept at the high price of *l'ecrevisse*

Many experienced hands involved in a Cajun boucherie. *Courtesy of Annette Huval.*

(crawfish) at home now that many recognize the versatility and deliciousness of this delicacy.

Laissez les bon temps roulez, or "Let the good times roll," a popular Cajun saying, expresses that despite trials and tribulations, the Cajuns are thrilled to conceive new festivals and prepare new dishes to celebrate life and embrace a unique heritage.

CRACKLING COOKING PARTY AT PALMETTO ISLAND STATE PARK

(PERRY)

This casual cooking demo of cracklings offers hot crispy samples to campers at beautiful Palmetto Island State Park. It's an annual event for local cooks to show off their skills in this 1,300-acre nature habitat along Vermilion River. Among nature trails, campsites, a boat launch, cabins and spots for bird watchers, live Cajun music plays throughout the day during this February event as bundles of cracklings are generously shared.

FETE DES BOUCHERS

(BATON ROUGE)

Chef John Folse takes a step back three hundred years to early life in Louisiana through his Fete des Bouchers held at his twenty-five-acre farm in Baton Rouge, White Oak Estate & Gardens. He is the owner of several food enterprises and hosts a nationally syndicated television cooking show called *A Taste of Louisiana*. Chef Folse is also the author of numerous cookbooks, including *The Encyclopedia of Cajun and Creole Cuisine*. The heavy tome is considered the bible of our food ways, detailing seven indigenous cultures that have influenced our cookery style in southwest Louisiana. Additionally, the Chef John Folse Culinary Institute of Nicholls State University in Thibodaux was opened in 1996 and named in his honor. In January 2020, Chef Folse received the Ella Brennan Lifetime Achievement award from the New Orleans Wine & Food Experience.

Of Cajun and German heritage, Chef Folse hails from St. James Parish, Louisiana, and was born on the 750-acre Cabanocey Plantation where his family was in the sugar industry. His down-to-earth style of outdoor cooking with black iron pots was inherited from his family, as he embraced the gifts of the Cajun culture. His gumbo has traveled the world through the Reagan-Gorbachev summit. In the early 1990s, he opened pop-up restaurants in London, Bogota, Taipei, Seoul and other international cities, where he introduced the ultimate comfort dish of gumbo to delighted fans. In 1989, he was the first non-Italian chef to create the Vatican State Dinner in Rome, where he served seafood gumbo to (Saint) Pope John Paul II.

Chef Folse has hosted the Fete des Bouchers, an annual gathering of seventy butchers and chefs from all over the United States, since 2016 to celebrate the art of butchery and cooking and to keep the ritual of boucheries alive. Before preparation of the dishes begins, a butcher's prayer is recited to laud the bounty of the animals.

Positioned at boucherie stations, the culinary comrades armed with spices and kitchen tools share their love of preparing such tasty dishes as smoked raccoon and rooster stew, freshly fried cracklings, rabbit and pork sauce piquante, backbone stew and white beans, ponce (stuffed pig stomach) and pork and sausage fricassee. Each pot holds a surprise. Peek inside one big pot as the hog's head and feet simmer, awaiting preparation of hogshead cheese as an appetizer. One chef briskly stirs what looks like

Hogshead cheese is a Cajun pâté. *Courtesy of Chef John Folse.*

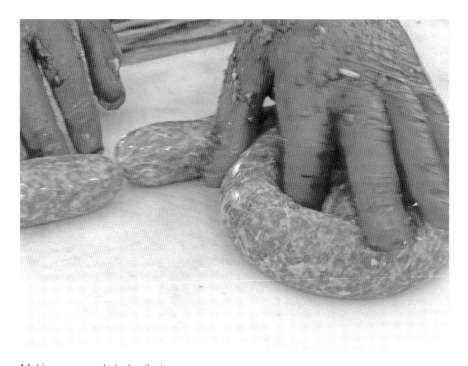

Making sausage. *Author's collection.*

a rich pudding. It's actually the pig's blood, a key ingredient in making boudin rouge or blood boudin. As chefs compare notes on cooking styles, they entertain questions and share recipes.

Following the butchering of the pig at a long wooden table, the chefs join in as a throwback to early days when Louisiana boucheries meant neighbors worked together to cook and preserve food. Meat from the pig was cut into roasts, pork chops and ribs. Hams were cured in sugar brine and smoked. Pig skin was boiled down to use in frying cracklings and making lard. Boudin and sausage were stuffed into casings.

Chef Folse's most recent fete sported a comical theme of "I Like Pig Butts and I Cannot Lie." The Fete des Bouchers includes demonstrations of curing meats and preparation of charcuterie platters. Tours of White Oak Estate & Gardens showcase Berkshire and Iron Age hogs, which can shoot up to six hundred pounds, fenced poultry yards of prized chickens and heritage turkeys, rabbits and a pond stocked with largemouth bass.

The farm includes a smokehouse topped with a weathervane of a pig. The Old Smokey Smokehouse was repurposed from its original role as a two-hole outhouse at Cabanocey Plantation and later moved to White Oak in 2005. It was then reconstructed into a smokehouse in which more than one thousand pounds of smoked meats can be prepared at one time.

The grand finale of the Fete is a "Spoils of the Boucherie" lunch, a mile-long spread of prime pork dishes and sides with the showpiece of a roasted pig.

FRENCH FOOD FESTIVAL

(Larose)

This foodie festival was originally called the Bouillabaisse Festival in South Lafourche and is now hosted every October in the town of Larose. This old-fashioned celebration features the best of Cajun cooking as well as a community art competition and folklife demonstrations. A one-of-a-kind dish is the Boucherie Burger, an Angus beef patty topped with pork grillades, bacon, cheese and cracklings.

GRAND HOORAH

(Ville Platte)

Held during blooming springtime at various locations in Acadiana, Le Grand Hoorah kicks off with a fiddle and ends with an accordion to celebrate Louisiana's cultural riches. The fest packs in a bit of school time, festival, jam sessions and family reunion that leads into Dewey Balfa Week, which is held at Chicot State Park in Ville Platte. The motto is "Jouer. Danser. Manger. Repeter," French for "Play, Dance, Eat, Repeat." Music and dance lessons are offered, a boucherie is hosted and top-notch bands play Cajun music. The event honors Dewey Balfa, a legendary accordionist from the town of Mamou.

JAMBALAYA FESTIVAL

(Gonzales)

The town was declared Jambalaya Capital of the World in 1967 through a festival. The inaugural fest pitted thirteen cooks against one another to be crowned "World Jambalaya Cooking Champion." Now every May, seventy cooks fine-tune their recipes for this popular one-pot dish of rice and meat. To make it appetizing, the meat thrown in the pot can be ham, chicken,

Jambalaya is a popular dish of rice and meats. *Courtesy of St. Landry Parish Tourist Commission.*

sausage, fresh pork, shrimp or oysters. Spices, wooden paddle and favorite black pot for cooking are just some of the tools and supplies that cooks stack up. Tons of jambalaya are cooked throughout the weekend. There are cook-offs, a car show, a jambalaya art show, a boxing contest, sky-diving exhibitions, sports tournaments and carnival rides.

PARKS CRACKLIN COOK-OFF

(PARKS)

It's held in the town of Parks on the weekend following Easter at the Cecile Rousseau Poche Memorial Park. For over forty-three years, this Friday through Sunday festival of live music, raffles, a poker run, a beer-drinking competition and an all-around good time have provided neighborly assistance to the community through a dedicated charity each year from the proceeds of the cook-off. Thirty teams set up in a shady spot to compete for best crackling on the block. As soon as the crispy bits are scooped out from hot pots and sprinkled with Cajun seasoning, spectators gobble them up. In local grocery stores, cracklings cost twenty dollars a pound and are served to-go in small paper bags. They can become addictive, whether biting into the soft spots or the crunchy part.

PORT BARRE CRACKLIN FESTIVAL

(PORT BARRE)

Port Barre is tagged as the "Birthplace of the Bayou Teche," as the town had its start in the early 1800s serving as a port as well as a French trading post. Every November since 1985, the Port Barre Lions Club has hosted this popular festival, with proceeds going to a charitable cause. A street fair, live music, a parade and a competition for the best cracklings are part of the fun.

T-shirts of Port Barre Crackling Festival. *Courtesy of St. Landry Parish Tourist Commission.*

SWINE FESTIVAL

(BASILE)

It's guaranteed that somebody is going to chase a pig at this festival held every November in Evangeline Parish. The Louisiana Swine Festival has celebrated ancestries of the swine industry in the local area since 1966. It's tied to the Louisiana Swine Association, founded in 1963 with the purpose of raising and selling feeder pigs in the Basile area. Queen Petunia and King Porky reign over festival events such as "A Pig's Tale" reading, hog education demonstrations, a boucherie demo, a hog calling contest and a boudin eating contest.

SMOKED MEATS FESTIVAL

(VILLE PLATTE)

With meat on the pit and producing delicious smokes since 1992, the Smoked Meats Festival dedicates its efforts to the local chapter of the Vietnam Veterans Association. Hosted by Viande Boucanee Inc. and Ville Platte Lions Club, the goal is to honor all military veterans. Bragging about the number of trophies that teams have won from the festival's championship cook-off is just part of the fun.

ST. JOHN THE BAPTIST PARISH ANDOUILLE FESTIVAL

(LaPLACE)

This October festival, held annually since 1972 in LaPlace, commemorates the area's French and German heritage. The technique of smoking andouille is similar to the days when the town was established in the early 1700s by German immigrants as part of Louisiana's "German Coast." Highlights of the festival include cooking competitions for gumbo, jambalaya and other dishes in which andouille is used. Aside from music, crafts and a beauty pageant, a special procession of a second line parade streams through festival grounds. This procession, which originated in New Orleans, stars a marching brass band with its members decked out in extravagant suits, hats and parasols. Although the energetic mix of jubilant singing, dancing and trumpets blaring are normally associated with funerals in which mourners follow, the colorful second line parade may also commemorate holidays and other celebrations.

VERMILIONVILLE COCHON DE LAIT

(LAFAYETTE)

On a brisk November morning, the grounds of Vermilionville, an eighteenth-century Acadian village, is covered with red and gold leaves. Veteran masters of swine and dine turn up at 6:00 a.m. to prepare to roast two fifty-pound suckling pigs. Demonstrations throughout the day share the ins and outs of pig roasts to keep the tradition alive. For this old-style cochon de lait, a butterflied pig with an apple in its mouth is roasted horizontally on an open makeshift pit. The pig is turned every few hours for consistent cooking until eight hours later, when the skin is crispy. Four fires, of which two are larger, are set under the pig and stoked to ensure even cooking. The backside of the pig, which bares the thicker part, is strategically placed over the two larger fires, as this side is thicker and will take longer to cook.

The other pig is cooked in the more modern process of an outdoor Cajun microwave. This ingenious cooker is basically a wooden box, usually of cypress wood, lined with sheet metal. To retain the heat, a metal cover is topped with hot charcoal. Heat radiates throughout the box for cooking the meat slowly and evenly. To prep the pig, it is seasoned with rub and also injected with liquid seasoning. There's a small tin box filled with apple cider for infusion to add a subtle taste to the pork. Cooking the pig in this method takes eight hours though there is no direct flame. The pig transforms into a riot of juicy mess, falling off the bone. As onlookers check the progress of both pig roasts, they are entertained by a Vermilionville artisan dressed in a country-style top hat and garb suitable for a Cajun village of the late 1700s. He livens up the scene by playing the accordion.

Sampling stations are set throughout the park for visitors to partake of representative dishes that would be enjoyed at a typical country cochon de lait. Boudin is prepared by Johnson's Boucaniere Restaurant with Lori and her father, Wallace, explaining how boudin is stuffed. At another station, a cover of a black iron pot is raised for a peek at beef cowboy stew. This dish has a musky smell and is made of cow kidney, liver and spleen. Pork cracklings are deep fried then scooped up for a brief cooling period, allowing time for the cooks to clean the cauldron and refill with cooking oil to fry a second time. It's the repeat performance of a second frying that is the key to success of a tasty batch of cracklings. The Cajun Pig's Ear Pastry or *oreilles de cochons* is similar to a Cajun fritter. It's a two-inch-wide strip of dough that is deep fried. By using a long fork, the dough is twisted into the shape of a pig's ear. A heated mix of Steen's cane syrup and chopped pecans is drizzled over the hot pastry. Other stations include sliced beef tongue, beef liver and onions and the Cajun standard of pork stew and white beans.

Vermilionville offers resources for learning more about the Acadian culture through regular events, summer camps, costumed craftspeople and artifacts. For educators, there is a lesson plan available detailing suggested activities and a glossary relating to communal boucheries.

WORLD CHAMPIONSHIP GUMBO COOK-OFF

(New Iberia)

Over twenty thousand people attend one of the biggest gumbo events in Louisiana. It's held in downtown New Iberia, near the Bayou Teche. Visitors are hopeful that the temperature will drop for the first day of the festival in keeping with the hot dish. Cooking competitions such as "Meanest Beans" honor camp-style cooking. Gumbo competitors are restricted from using pre-prepared jarred roux. Cooks are required to make their own roux on site and tote in the ingredients of flour and vegetable oil, as well as their favorite wooden spoon for stirring. They must be skilled in the know-how of stirring a roux without letting it burn. As a fundraiser for the New Iberia Chamber of Commerce, the first cook-off began over thirty years ago with only twenty booths and has grown to more than one hundred teams who keep the flame going to prepare seafood, chicken or a third category of mélange, which can range from duck to gator.

6

PIGGY TALES OF LOCAL LOVERS OF PORK

Still, round the corner, there may wait, A new road or a secret gate.
—*J.R.R. Tolkien*

Hit the open road to visit the nooks, crannies, bayous and forests of Louisiana. When you cruise through a one-stoplight town, don't hurry through. Enjoy planning a road trip cross-country or just across the road. As my grandparents may have said, "Take a buggy ride and see some people."

Here are some ideas for small-town adventures in the Bayou State. Along the countryside, you may spot handmade signs of "Baby Rabbits for Sale" and a few miles later "Stop for Homemade Quilts" and, finally, near the four-way stop, "Ain't Nothin' for Sale Here." Discover ladies in waiting at the D-Lux Beauty Shop sharing space with the Hammer Away hardware store in a building from the 1940s that pours free Community Coffee and stocks shiny tools, kitchen aprons, gumbo spoons and yard eggs. These adventures of snaking around the bend may include the following:

- Ride your bike on country roads.
- Take a hike to explore the outdoors.
- Fill up your bucket at a blueberry farm.
- Get your fishing pole out, pack a picnic lunch and head to the best spots along the coast.
- Stroll downtown sidewalks for a bird's-eye view of first-place garden club flowerbeds.

Oyster shells. *Courtesy of Annette Huval.*

Alligators may be found in many Louisiana bayous. *Courtesy of Annette Huval.*

- Get a local history lesson by walking through an old cemetery.
- Cheer little leaguers at a summertime baseball game.
- Pretend you're Scarlett O'Hara in *Gone with the Wind* and wine and dine at a plantation home.
- Spend the night at a cabin in the woods and look up at the stars.
- Get drawn in by neon signs at local breweries to wet your whistle.

And take a seat at the shiny lunch counter to watch cooks prepare the best home-grown dishes. Listen to the chitchat and hobnob with diners enjoying the blue-plate special. These hole-in-the-wall joints or masters of haute cuisine offer spectacular nibbles and exceptional memories of porcine delights.

ALUMNI GRILL

1130 Highway 1 • Thibodaux, LA

Steeped in history, Thibodaux is a college town situated along Bayou Lafourche. The college, Nicholls State University, founded in 1948, was named after former Louisiana governor Francis T. Nicholls. The campus was once part of a historic sugar plantation called Acadia Plantation developed by legendary frontiersman James "Jim" Bowie, who served and died in the Battle of Alamo and lent his name to the Bowie knife.

Just a short distance from this historic district is an old-school eatery, Alumni Grill. Mark the spot for a good starting point "up the bayou" for grabbing good eats.

Especially popular at this casual restaurant are the hamburgers, which earn a blue ribbon for taste. Chef/Owner Minh Le left his native land of Vietnam at age seven, eventually moving to New Orleans with cousins. Due to immigration complications, he was placed with an American foster family by Catholic Charities and attended St. Paul's School in Covington. While a teenager, he was drawn to Louisiana's Northshore region where he worked part-time in a seafood restaurant.

Although testing new flavors and ingredients in the kitchen was a youthful interest, he moved to Lafayette, Louisiana, to pursue a degree in dietetics. In time, he followed the mantra of "be true to yourself," chasing his true passion of culinary arts by moving to Thibodaux, Louisiana, where he graduated from the John Folse Culinary Institute, an academic college of Nicholls State University. After hands-on learning the tools of the trade and diving into a gamut of duties in various restaurants in Baton Rouge and New Orleans, he formed his own kitchen, opening Alumni Grill in 2015.

The eatery's two dining rooms are large enough to seat an entire Little League baseball team, fresh from a win and ready to chow down on mile-high burgers that are packed with a punch. The Cardinal Burger is loaded with a beef patty, barbecue brisket and bacon stacked on a brioche bun. Alumni Grill is also famous for its jumbo pork sandwich overstuffed with oak-smoked pulled pork as well as flash-fried barbecue ribs and brisket sandwiches. Save room for dessert, such as King Cake milkshakes or tasty bread pudding.

The tongue-in-cheek appetizer Lard of the Fries includes smoked pork, bacon, barbecue sauce, cheddar and pepper jack cheeses and jalapeños covering crisp French fries. Once in a blue moon, an Asian dish such as bánh mì, a sandwich of meats and pickled vegetables served on a soft baguette, is introduced to diners. Bánh is Vietnamese for "bread."

Chef Le enjoys greeting customers while asking for feedback on the dishes he has created. Setting up and cooking in the kitchen lends him a sense of comfort. Taking short road trips to New Orleans to sample new dishes is a favorite pastime.

BAYOU TECHE BREWERY

1094 Bushville Highway • Arnaudville, LA

On nearly every street corner in the town of Arnaudville, you can eavesdrop on French conversations, and that's how the Cajun French roots are honored in this neck of the woods. With a population of 1,500, Arnaudville has become a popular destination for cyclists as they ease through scenic roads to enjoy a view of the junction of two waterways, the Bayou Teche and Bayou Fuselier. A fair number of goats and chickens mingle along the countryside. Down the road, families are holding hands as they fill a bucket of berries at a blueberry farm. Downtown, the fiddle shop hosts regular jam sessions and provides music lessons. Cajun arts, specifically dance, music and culture, are preserved by a community initiative called NuNu's. In an effort to sustain the francophone community, "French tables" are hosted for those who speak French to gather for conversation with discussions covering football scores, politics and quilt making. Arnaudville retains its homespun setting with a couple of restaurants and a snowball stand. You can count on an Etouffee Festival every spring. Etouffee is French for the cooking style of "smothering a dish," as in crawfish, cabbage or pork.

Amid all of this is the Bayou Teche Brewery, which brews a variety of twenty-five beers for the locals and visitors who are savvy enough to take the short detour off I-10.

A few years ago, the Knott family brainstormed about developing a brewery based on their passion for beer. Stationed in Germany courtesy of the U.S. Army for six years, Karlos Knott popped into several pubs to sample regional beers along the line of malty pale lagers, wheat beer and dark beer made with rye. Upon his return to Louisiana, Karlos embraced the hobby of making his own beer by experimenting step-by-step with processes and tastes.

While enjoying a pitcher of homemade beer in which they agreed that the recipe had finally been perfected, brothers Karlos, Dorsey and Byron sketched out a business plan for opening their own brewery. On St. Patrick's Day 2010, they toasted mugs of their homemade brew in pursuit of crafting a unique beer. Their plan was to concoct the right beer blends to complement the abundance of Cajun dishes they were raised on. They appreciated that homeowners would be drawn to sample unique beer. They were also betting that their style of beer would attract a wider population. In a converted discarded railroad car into a farmhouse brewery on family property near Arnaudville, Bayou Teche Brewery was born.

Encased in casual surroundings, a canopy of trees shades a covered patio and beer garden lined with picnic tables adjacent to the brewery to accommodate weekend gatherings with entertainment by Cajun bands. A taproom for ordering a flight of cold beer accommodates choices of light or dark beer. The magic of making beer is revealed through weekend tours guided by retired educator and family patriarch Floyd Knott. A Boudreaux and Thibodeaux joke, comingling English and French, is given when Floyd leads Saturday brewery tours. He's the man to set you straight about what an IPA is as he guides visitors through the science of beer making. Brewery special events include a boucherie held on Black Friday and a cochon de lait in early springtime.

The flagship beer for the Knott brothers is Bière Pâle, symbolized by the green LA31 label or tap handle. Classified by the brewery as a Louisiana

Pale Ale, this is the beer the Knotts designed to pair with local dishes. Using Belgian malts and American hops and yeast, the bronze-colored LA31 Bière Pâle is a unique brew to mirror Acadian tastes. Other beers include Passionné, a wheat beer with a bright citrus flavor of passion fruit; and a "rye" spicy beer called Saison D'Ecrevisses. The majority of the beers developed by Bayou Teche Brewery are available on tap or in tall bottles that are distributed throughout Louisiana and Texas and Quebec, Canada.

According to the Chinese zodiac, 2019 was the year of the pig, making this an ingenious time for the brewery to launch a Cajun Breakfast Stout made with local boudin from Russell's Food Center in Arnaudville, Steen's cane syrup from Abbeville and a local coffee brewed by Art's Coffee in Carencro. The boudin beer, as it's tagged, is a spin on a common Cajun breakfast where a link of boudin drizzled in cane syrup is juggled in one hand and a steaming cup of joe is grasped in the other.

The farm-to-table concept is realized, as local resources are used every step of the way to make this special beer. Just when you think that there is nothing new that can be done with boudin, this creation debuts. As part of the process, cane syrup and boudin are added to the mash early in the brewing process. Additional boudin links are added at the end of the boiling process. During the end of fermentation, coffee is added. This dark beer is

Cajun Breakfast Stout Beer. *Courtesy of Bayou Teche Brewery.*

Boudin is a handy snack of pork and rice. *Courtesy of St. Landry Parish Tourist Commission.*

not subtle; it exudes the taste of an interesting blend of spices from boudin, the slight sweetness of syrup and a definite hint of coffee.

To accompany the production of twenty-five distinct flavors of beer, the Bayou Teche Brewery has introduced Cajun Saucer Pizza baked in a wood-fired oven. Carnivores will enjoy the Streetcar Named Diablo Pizza with andouille, tasso, chaurice, smoked sausage and fried pork skins on top, complemented with a Sriracha honey drizzle.

BON CREOLE LUNCH COUNTER

1409 EAST ST. PETER STREET • NEW IBERIA, LA

Bon Creole ranks as the ultimate road tripper's discovery. New Iberia is a charming town with a showcase of itinerary choices. History buffs enjoy the Shadows, a red-brick 1834 house surrounded by towering live oak trees draped with Spanish moss along the banks of the Bayou Teche. Nearby tours are held of world-famous Tabasco® factory, where the pepper sauce is made. A few steps away is Jungle Gardens of Avery Island and Bird City, where self-guided tours introduce visitors to alligators in the wild, exotic botanical specimens from around the world and a private bird sanctuary for the once endangered snowy egret. An introduction to the mixed bag of nature and a glimpse into the past of New Iberia are not complete without stopping by one of the culinary hidden gems of the area.

Housed in a rectangular cinderblock building with the feel of a 1960s roadhouse, Bon Creole is identifiable by a faded mural of a giant crawfish painted on the front of the building. The interior has a windowless dining area with a hunting camp décor. It includes an eclectic collection of mounted deer heads, a full-sized wild turkey (the fowl, not the whiskey) and a buffalo head, too. The entourage of wildlife reflects owner/cook Randy Montegut's hobby of enjoying the great outdoors. The façade also includes a makeshift tin roof fastened to a wall and stacked with a nutria trap to complete the illusion of a Louisiana swamp scene. Montegut was trained at LSU as a fisheries biologist. He opened Bon Creole in 1982 initially as a crawfish processing operation, where he spent many hours peeling and packing crawfish tails. In 1995, he turned the business into a restaurant. Montegut sidelines by selling bowfin caviar from the fish we know locally as choupique, pronounced "shoe-pick," from the nearby Atchafalaya Basin.

Dining tabletops are crafted of old holey wood, adding to the rustic setting. It's well known that you're not heading to this joint for the atmosphere; you're coming for the well-seasoned, delicious dishes.

A cluttered counter stacked with community announcements overlooks the kitchen. The magic of cooking is performed by workers who are often singing or yelling customers' names when their order is ready. Most of the hungry patrons lining up have no need to look up at the posted menu, as many are repeat customers. Conversations center on news about the Sugar Cane Festival, how the fishing is going at nearby Cypremort Point, what play is being performed at the IPAL Theater and what the plot of the new book by native son James Lee Burke is about.

Fried food is the preferred fare: shrimp, oyster, catfish or crawfish served in a basket, on a salad or in an overstuffed poboy encased in a crunchy French bread loaf. Be forewarned, even the half-sized poboy is filling and dressed just right. Wait in line for the comfort food of chicken and sausage or seafood gumbo. Aside from what's on the menu, plate lunches are prepared on weekdays, such as the proverbial Monday favorite red beans and rice and Tuesday's entrée of pork roast. For the after-church crowd on Sundays, Bon Creole cooks barbecue ribs, chicken, pork chops and brisket.

Foodies quickly became crazed with Bon Creole's tantalizing dishes through the many festivals in which the eatery's bread bowl drips with creamy crawfish and spinach. Attendees of the Festivals International in Lafayette and the Breaux Bridge Crawfish Festival have praised the Bon Creole bread boat for over ten years, as for many, it's their first taste of crawfish. And so the addiction began!

BOURGEOIS MEAT MARKET

543 West Main Street • Thibodaux, LA

With a heritage tied to boucheries, the Bourgeois family of Thibodaux has created a boudin dynasty of four generations involved in the process of making boudin, as well as a couple of other Cajun specialties since 1891.

At the end of the nineteenth century, Valerie Jean-Baptiste Bourgeois, with sharp cleaver in hand and a homemade wooden chopping block, used his butchering skills to perfect prime cuts for customers. He traveled by horse and wagon on dusty roads, stopping house to house to sell his wares. Faced with the lack of refrigeration at home, he did not return to greet his family until nearly every wrapped piece of meat was sold.

His son, Lester, continued in the family profession of butchery arts in a new storefront and slaughterhouse, which was built next to the family home along the bayou in the early 1920s. Under his direction, the store building was moved across the street to give more space for parking. At one

The Bourgeois men comprise a dynasty of boudin makers in Thibodaux. *Courtesy of Cajun Food Trail.*

Delivering groceries by buggy. *New York Public Library.*

time, the store's coolers were stocked with beef, pork and chicken. But as supermarkets opened in the region, Bourgeois specialized in pork and calf meat. Lester perfected his methods of making hogshead cheese and smoked sausage through a homemade smokehouse.

Drafted into World War II at age eighteen, Lester was stationed in India. He filled his free time with being entertained by a pet monkey during his stint as a radio operator. One of Lester's critical roles was to monitor cargo planes filled with weapons and fuel flying from India to China across the Himalayas.

Now ninety-four and semiretired, Lester "Paw Paw" Bourgeois visits the family meat market daily to give his experienced advice to the market crew, sometimes riding his bicycle, as he lives nearby. His days are also filled with fishing, especially at the nearby town of DesAllemands. Weekly lunches with his buddies, the "Has Beans," all aged ninety plus, are on his agenda. Afternoons often end with popping open a cold beer while sitting on the front porch of his house.

The family house he was born in and continues to enjoy was built as a cypress carriage house in 1853. He reminisces about earlier days when his family had a huge home garden that included a sizable crop of corn suitable for fattening up the hogs. A family dog was trained to herd the hogs and cows on the farm. Wooden fences were not always reliable for keeping the livestock from trampling through the garden, and the family depended on fresh vegetables to provide side dishes.

Enter third-generation Donald Bourgeois to the business. Following his graduation with a business degree from Nicholls State University, he continued his involvement in the family meat market. His claim to fame was an amazing dream he had—not a vision, it was an actual dream. His dream concerned a hot-ticket item to offer to customers. Since there was an influx of Mexican restaurants opening in the area, he wanted to come up with a specialty tied to Cajun cuisine as well as Mexican dishes. What would happen if he scooped a few spoonfuls of the meat normally prepared for the Bourgeois boudin? His dream came true by filling a tortilla with boudin meat and, voila, creating the popular Bourgeois Boudin Burrito.

He also experimented with making beef jerky through Bourgeois's ever-growing smokehouse. Leftover bits of extra-lean steak that are too small to use for jerky are ground and stuffed into a skinny casing and then hung up for smoking. These wiry beef "styx" are good for snacking. They're seasoned and marinated for twenty-four hours and hung from nails on long rails. The styx are placed in a smokehouse designed by patriarch Valerie Bourgeois and smoked all day to ensure flavor, texture and color. No nitrates or artificial smoke flavorings are added.

Look out for fourth-generation Beau Bourgeois, who had absolutely no plans to carry on the boudin dynasty. He graduated from Nicholls State University with a degree in computer science. He attended Tulane University in New Orleans in the PhD program and earned his master's degree in math. Then all roads seemed to lead back to Thibodaux, and he returned home, overjoyed to join the family business.

Beau walks tall with the experiences of three generations behind him. He knows his way through the smokehouse, coolers and chopping block, all the while greeting customers and working the front counter. As a lad, his first job was answering the phone and vacuum packing beef jerky. He enjoys his weekly (or is it daily?) taste of rice and gravy, noting that his favorite cut are the neck chops because they make the best gravy. Explaining the cuts is second nature to him because he knows the animal parts. Oxtail, also considered a cow's tail, is a delicacy that is unexpectedly useful for cooking mock turtle soup. The meat market produces a lighter blond crackling made from the back fat part of the pig. Cracklings are time consuming to cook, which explains the normally high pricing in many meat markets that use a different part of the pig, such as belly fat. The process of preparing

A link of hot boudin for breakfast or lunch. *Courtesy of Cajun Food Trail.*

this popular crunchy treat is time intensive, normally taking two hours to monitor the hot oil for frying the crackling bits twice.

More customers will be enjoying the bounty of foodstuffs, as Bourgeois Meat Market is introducing a second location nearby, within the community of Gray. Customers stop by with their grocery list and ask advice from Beau about the weather. Is gumbo weather around the bend? What's best to add to it? Patrons include oil field salesmen en route to Fourchon and fishermen stocking up for early mornings at Grand Isle.

The Bourgeois staff prepares boudin blanc (white boudin) at least twice a week beginning as early as 2:00 a.m. Likely the team has the radio blaring "Gotta Make a Living, He's a Louisiana Man," as musician Doug Kershaw wrote. It takes two people to stir the giant black iron pot, which boils for hours. It's filled with deboned chunks from various pig parts, including the liver and intestines. All pig parts are important, as they add distinctive tastes. Once meat is tender, it's scooped out with shovels to transport to the cutting table. The process continues as the meat is run through a grinder and mixed with seasoning, green onions and cooked rice. It's a hands-on process with miles and miles of boudin links stuffed into casing. For seafood lovers, crawfish boudin is produced and snatched up during the Lenten season, when many Catholics abstain from eating meat on Fridays.

Among the tally of goodies Bourgeois prepares is blood boudin (boudin rouge) with a distinctive dark color and earthy taste. In the old days of boucheries, the pig was hung, killed and its throat slit while a pail was placed underneath to catch the blood to use in making the unique boudin. Salt was added to keep it from coagulating. Nowadays, the pig's blood is boiled as an early step in preparing this specialty boudin. The State of Louisiana tightened restrictions on making blood boudin, causing slaughterhouses, butchers and meat markets in Lafourche Parish to discontinue making it years ago. However, Bourgeois studied the process and took two years to develop an efficient and safe process. The 1970s meat inspection act refined the process of making blood boudin.

Pork lovers unite in their quest for the perfect boudin, smoked sausage or cracklings. The Bourgeois clan carries on, as the authentic smokehouse designed by Valerie Jean-Baptiste Bourgeois continues to smoke meats the old-fashioned way.

CAFÉ JOSEPHINE

818 Napoleon Avenue • Sunset, LA

The little town of Sunset began as a railroad hub in the early 1900s. Art galleries, a Saturday morning farmer's market, antique shops and an annual Herbs and Gardens Festival make this a peaceful setting for strolling downtown. Look upward, as sunrises and sunsets in this picturesque spot are memorable. The town is also home to a pre–Civil War mansion, Chretien Point, the site of an 1863 battle. It seems that just about every town boasts that it's the world capital of something unusual. Sunset is tagged as "Rubboard Capital of the World" and commemorates a regional musical instrument of corrugated metal that is used when playing zydeco music. A rubboard, also called a washboard, adds to the flavor of a lively tempo. It's also known as a *frottoir* in French, which means "scrubbing."

Tucked away on Napoleon Street in Sunset is Café Josephine. The name of the restaurant is a reference to Napoleon Bonaparte's wife, Josephine. Converting an eighty-year-old square concrete block into a café was just one of many challenges that Chef Troy Bijeaux faced.

His career has spanned from working in the oilfield industry to installing and finishing wooden floors to running a meat market. Though he never formally attended culinary school, he loves his time in the kitchen to blend spices and use fresh ingredients. He demonstrated his prowess by creating tasty plate lunches and gourmet pizza at the meat market, which he operated for two years at this same site. As customers raved about his sleight of hand at the stove, Chef Troy was convinced to upgrade to a fine-dining eatery by modifying the façade of the building.

The café is easy on the eyes, with an old-timey atmosphere of pressed tin ceilings, fresh flowers at each table, concrete floors and the showpiece of a glassed-in oyster bar featuring antique pastel-tinted oyster dishware. Oyster lovers may take their pick from raw or charbroiled. The menu offers a good mix for both lunch and dinner. Dress up fancy or pull up to the parking lot on your bicycle, and you'll feel at home. At dinnertime, the place is at full tilt.

Sunset, Louisiana, is the Rubboard Capital of the World. *Courtesy of St. Landry Parish Tourist Commission.*

Chef Troy enjoys crafting home-cooked dishes while adding some sizzle. The "Trio Fajita" dish, good for sharing, is a mix of prime rib-eye, braised pork belly, smoked duck breast and wild mushrooms. The "Big Pork Chop" is grilled in orange juice and topped with fig sauce. Ham, bacon and tasso used in the specialty dishes are smoked in-house.

CITY PORK BRASSERIE & BAR

7227 JEFFERSON HIGHWAY • BATON ROUGE, LA

City Pork offers piggy morsels from brunch time through dinner in a snazzy setting, geared toward socializing. Charcuterie boards flaunt a hogshead cheese spread accompanied with smoky revelations of house-smoked andouille, truffle sausage and pastrami. Small plates entice with pork debris poutine, a filling side dish with pickled jalapeños, smoked cheddar and giblet gravy. Originating in Canada, poutine is a junk food dish of French fries and cheese curds usually topped with brown gravy.

Hungry diners can't resist the call of the wild with Wild Boar Flautas. Flour tortillas are loaded with coffee- and chile-braised pork and fried crunchy with a tender filling. Other menu choices include boudin balls, cured duck bacon salad, hamburgers, seafood, rabbit or lamb.

Early starts to your day begin with a plate of jaw-dropping cochon de lait eggs benedict with a nice surprise of an egg served on Texas toast. It's topped with pulled pork, smoked cheddar cheese and a Cajun hollandaise sauce. The fixins of the City Pork Bacon Bloody Mary include a strip or two of in-house cured bacon along with spices.

Lunchtime welcomes a pork belly hoagie on a platter. Chefs recognize the versatility of hog belly, also tagged as the underside, as richly flavored fatty layers. The hoagie filler goes through four crazy cooking techniques of smoking, searing, braising and deep frying to complete the coffee-braised pork sandwich, served with mustard greens. Another tasty sandwich is the Cubano of pulled pork, house-cured ham, swiss cheese and mojo sauce on Cuban bread.

For the ultimate pork lovers, there's baby back ribs with honey bourbon peaches and a tomahawk pork chop with duck cornbread dressing. The andouille-stuffed quail features the roasted fowl packed with andouille stuffing and covered with a light splattering of blackberry bourbon demi glaze.

City Pork has a second location on the campus of the Fighting Tigers of Louisiana State University. Weddings, holidays and LSU tailgating are all special events where City Pork Catering will bring out a whole roasted pig and all of the Southern sides for an authentic cochon de lait.

CORMIER'S CREOLE KITCHEN

303 MAIN STREET • GUEYDAN, LA

The town of Gueydan (pronounced gay dawn) is a nature lover's haven. When duck season opens in autumn, waterfowl hunters travel in droves for a weekend getaway to the camp. In eager anticipation, they search for the elusive speckle berry goose while enjoying a natural setting and trudging through rainy, cold weather. The retreat also serves as a time of camaraderie among hunters. Eerie cries of geese at the crack of dawn give hope for a successful bagging of a limit of ducks.

One downtown fixture for good eats on the way to hunters' paradise, Cormier's Creole Kitchen, has been catering to crowds since 1948, when it opened as a billiard hall. As folks racked up pool sticks and cued up, the cook griddled fat, juicy hamburgers. Keeping it simple, the business gradually reinvented itself as a full-service restaurant. Old-fashioned booths and dining tables were added along with a big-screen TV for watching sports events.

Rice and sugar cane farmers belly up to the counter for the daily plate lunch of rice and gravy as they gab about the state of their upcoming harvests. Waitresses barrel out of the kitchen with trays of barbecue sausage and pulled pork. Beef tongue with rice and gravy is served on special occasions. Duck hunters hoping to bag their limit of mergansers are treated to breakfast specials of "Duck Hunters" and "Goose Hunters" with variations of biscuit, eggs and meat choices. The hiss of the deep fryers at work can be heard as battered shrimp are dropped in for preparing poboys. On the road every fall, Cormier's crew loads up a modified, supersized food truck to work the nearby Crowley Rice Festival by sharing the fruits of home cooking.

Hunting season is a busy time at the eatery, so is Mardi Gras. An active carnival season is celebrated in Gueydan through parades and other special events. The Gueydan Duck Festival held in the fall is over forty years old. That's when the pintail and the Louisiana *poule d'eau*, French for "water chicken" and also known as the American coot, are honored. The festival includes duck and goose calling contests and dog trials as a show of how man and his best friend work together.

Rambling through downtown Gueydan is like walking through the streets of a quiet little hamlet like Mayberry from the old Andy Griffith Show. Across the street from Cormier's is a two-storied red-brick building from 1902. Once a bank, the majestic structure houses the Gueydan Museum, which hosts special events and an exhibit dedicated to the Gueydan Duck Festival.

Gueydan was founded in the late 1800s on marshy land by Jean-Pierre Gueydan of France. It became an important rail hub for rice farmers. Nearby is the White Lake Wetlands Conservation Area with its birding and nature trail.

LA CUISINE DE MAMAN AT VERMILIONVILLE

300 Fisher Road • Lafayette, LA

You may search the world for the best dishes only to discover that they are situated in your own backyard. What could be better than grandma's cooking? The little café located in Vermilionville packs a punch of home-style cooking.

Iconic Cajun vittles such as a flavorful gumbo with sausage chunks and chicken bits bobbing, red beans and sausage and rice, fried pork chops and roasted pork loin are available on the menu or served on a lunchtime buffet line. A heaping plateful of chicken and sausage jambalaya offers a spicy treat sided with sweet potato biscuits. Lunch is reasonably priced and satisfying, and the mood is inviting. The only thing missing to remind you of home is a well-worn gingham apron hanging on a kitchen peg. Settling in at a table near the floor-to-ceiling glass windows provides a bird's-eye view overlooking Acadian-style buildings. It's worth spending a day at this twenty-three-acre folklife park reminiscent of the nineteenth century along the Bayou Vermilion.

This twenty-year-old living history museum offers a treasure-trove of experiences to sample the richness of local cuisine and culture. Because it preserves the vast elements of folklife cultures in Louisiana such as Acadian, Creole, Native American and African, visitors are treated to nineteen attractions. History is definitely hands-on at the seven restored original homes. Costumed artisans are stationed throughout the park to demonstrate a past way of life through quilting, spinning, weaving, healing with medicinal herbs, boudin making and more. Many of the buildings are supplied with period kitchen tools, hand-carved decoys, clothing and farm implements. Get your dancing shoes out to stomp to the music of alternating live Cajun or zydeco music performed in the complex at the Le Bal du Dimanche Sunday dance. Special events, group tours or school field trips are available year-round.

EAST GATE BBQ

7516 Highway 182 East • Morgan City, LA

123 La Neuville Road • Youngsville, LA

A set of high school classmates with a South Louisiana twang have created an interesting combination of Texas-style barbecue. A wood-burning grill creates some hot stuff, like brisket egg rolls.

Their "psycho pig" dish is served on toasted onion rolls. "Legendary" is what owners Harlan Kappel and Chad Daigle call it, from a concoction of pulled pork and homemade buffalo sauce stacked with grilled onions and jalapeños and drizzled with ranch dressing. It's all jam-packed on a toasted onion roll.

Both guys were influenced by their restaurant families growing up. Harlan spent some time in Texas, where he perfected slow-smoked barbecue meats while Chad fashioned a tiny boiled seafood joint serving a crazy contrast of hot boiled crawfish and cold snowballs.

Their business was named after the East Gate Shopping Center in Morgan City, which Harlan's grandfather built. The creative chefs have progressed from their days of using a Cajun microwave, a metal box used to barbecue, which defined their first backyard culinary arts experiment.

Now ribs are prepped with their own rub of sugar, garlic, cayenne pepper and perhaps the kitchen sink before the ribs are smoked for three hours. The bundle is worked over again by a tight wrapping and smoked for yet a second go-round. The finish line makes them tender enough to fall off the bones. Turkeys, pork shoulders and ham are smoked during the holidays for takeaway and sided with meaty rice dressing.

Their Big Slop Sandwich mixes brisket, pulled pork and sausage cooked down with East Gate's own barbecue sauce. It's dressed with coleslaw and pepper jack cheese until juices drip down your chin as your teeth sink in. A bit of nostalgia is served through the Pulled Pork Frito Pie: a bed of corn chips topped with cheeses and chili and finished with a smattering of pulled pork.

The menu item called Trash Grits is a variation of grits and debris. Debris is made by combining the leftover parts of the pig, such as the liver and intestines, and cooking it down.

ELSIE'S PLATE & PIE

3145 GOVERNMENT STREET • BATON ROUGE, LA

This sassy eatery in Louisiana's capital city resembles a canteen and is sandwiched between cottages and a cool dive bar. Patrons cycle around or stroll through, looking for top-notch food served in a charming spot.

The namesake for the shop was inspired by owner/chef Paul Dupré's grandmother. He named the café in her honor and incorporated many of her dishes. A portrait of Elsie Marie Campeau Rupe of Lafourche Parish greets customers at the entrance. The eatery flaunts its open-air mix of modern industrial chic with old-school galley styling. Counters are shiny, and dining tabletops are made from worn cabinet doors. Elsie's is a tip-top place for coffee or a cocktail during brunch, lunch or dinner.

The menu delights with its eclectic mix of Southern comfort food such as red beans and rice or gumbo for winter days. A sweet special is the grilled honey-brined bone-in pork chop splattered with blueberry pepper jelly BBQ sauce. The boudin burger is stacked high with a juicy hamburger patty and a boudin patty, loaded with pepper jack and smoked gouda cheeses with a topping of pepper jelly. An appealing twist on a seafood dish, the crawfish queso is sided with pork skins to use for dipping rather than traditional nacho chips. The menu takes grilled cheese sandwiches to a whole other level with its remarkable melts. Salads, poboys and fancier entrées offer more deluxe choices.

Chef Dupré treasures the times he spent in his grandmother's kitchen along with seven other grandchildren and thirteen great-grandchildren rolling out dough to bake pies. The main draw at Elsie's is the unforgettable home-baked pies, both savory like the famous busting-at-the-seams Natchitoches meat pie with beef and pork. The pork and sweet potato pie takes sweet taters to a whole new level. The pie includes tender braised pork shoulder in a succulent gravy and is topped with fluffy sweet potatoes. It's garnished with a medley of stewed greens and a cane-soy glaze.

For a slice of sweets, you may be hard-pressed to choose between Almond Joy Pie, pistachio cream pie with pomegranate whip, root beer float pie and blackberry margarita pie, in addition to your retro apple pie. "Sweet" nachos are fashioned with strips of a flaky pie crust that are lightly fried and drizzled with a heavenly fresh fruit puree. If your to-do list includes preparing dessert for a potluck supper, whole luscious pies are available for pickup.

THE EUNICE SUPERETTE

1230 West Laurel • Eunice, LA

Slow down as you drive through Eunice, as this charming town offers quirky layers to a road trip that should not be missed. There's a college, namely LSUE; the Liberty Theater, which is a 1924 vaudeville house now hosting Cajun music on a regular basis; signage supporting the Bobcats, the mascot of the local high school; and even more curious aspects of the Cajun prairieland.

Mardi Gras is celebrated in a high-spirited way in Eunice. The Courir de Mardi Gras or Running of the Mardi Gras is a country celebration in which bands of masked riders on horseback or in wagons travel from house to house. Dressed in homemade tattered costumes, the frenzied Mardi Gras riders are comrades who faithfully follow their captain through the countryside searching for necessary ingredients to cook a gumbo. They entertain by performing antics as they hunt for rice, pork sausage (or the whole hog) and a chicken.

In the midst of this merriment stands the iconic statue of a giant black cow standing atop the Eunice Superette. The store's T-shirts flaunt "Put Some South in Ya Mouth," promoting the varieties of meats in this superstore of Cajun fare. "Ici on parle francais" says a sign at the entryway, proudly proclaiming that "French is spoken here."

Eunice native Jerome Moore opened a superstore and slaughterhouse in 1962 to provide groceries and meats to locals. A few miles away from the current location of the Superette is the slaughterhouse, which still prepares livestock and wild game for supermarkets, restaurants and butcher shops. It's the go-to place for ordering a pig for your weekend roast and is considered Louisiana's largest meat-processing facility.

A bonanza of meats and specialty items, the Superette opens at the crack of dawn as a one-stop shop for commuters planning for breakfast on the go as they crave boudin or crackling. Or try a variation of a boudin wrap, which places a pyramid of traditional boudin meat mounted with a chunk of pepper jack cheese and cradled in an eggroll wrapper, all fried until crispy.

All day long, visitors turn up to take a nickel tour of the shop and poke around the variety of goods. "What exactly is a boo-dan? It looks a bit like the sausage we prepare for bangers and mash," questioned a British customer who was taking in the wonderful aroma in the store. Another customer from the parish happily explained that boudin is a Cajun

Right: The Courir de Mardi Gras is part of the Cajun culture. *Courtesy of Roby Poché.*

Below: The Eunice Superette is a 1962 favorite spot for meats of all kinds. *Courtesy of St. Landry Parish Tourist Commission.*

trademark, similar to sausage. "You slow-cook pork from various parts of the pig, grind it and mix it with cooked white rice. Add some spices and vegetables like onions. Once it's all mixed, you stuff the jumble in a casing, and it's ready to go out the door."

Wandering customers armed with small ice chests are given advice on how to use the stockpile showcased in self-service coolers. Do you grill it, roast it or cook it in a stew? It's hog heaven to find such a variety of brisket, injected bacon-wrapped pork tenderloin, smoked turkey tasso and bags of bacon chunks. Pig's ears, pig's feet and ham hocks—the entire setup is ideal for adding meaty pizazz to a pot of red beans and rice. Scratch your head at the wide range of choices you have in crackling variety, pig or chicken. Line up at the wonderland of meats and fill up your basket with lamb chops or beef tongue or the whole head of a hog.

FRANCIS SMOKEHOUSE & SPECIALTY MEATS
FRANCIS SOUTHERN TABLE & BAR

6779 US-61 · St. Francisville, LA

One of the most scenic and historic areas of southeast Louisiana is the Felicianas (means "happy land" in Spanish), made famous for the time that artist and naturalist John James Audubon spent teaching art in 1821 and also where he painted thirty-two of his *Birds of America* masterpieces. The region draws bird lovers, cyclists and history enthusiasts. Although a hop, skip and a jump north of Cajun Country, there's one popular specialty meat market that prepares the Cajun favorites of boudin and crackling along with some mean barbecue. Meats in cold boxes such as boudin-stuffed quail and ribs are ready to grill. The hot box has boudin balls, fried chicken and chicken wings ready for snacking.

Picnic tables are set near the entrance of the shop. The spot is dog-friendly, and the scent of the smokehouse working overtime hits you when the shop opens at 10:00 a.m., for it's the only game in town for boudin. Plate lunches with a special jumble of pork stew with rice and gravy goes out the door quickly.

Next door is a cushier eatery. Handing out a full menu of steak, seafood and salads, the Francis Southern Table & Bar is a kissing cousin to the Francis

Crispy pig skin cracklings. *Courtesy of St. Landry Parish Tourist Commission.*

Smokehouse. Occasionally, a band plays as music lovers enjoy the outdoor patio with an alluring setting of an oak tree canopy.

After visitors enjoy a meal in town, many opportunities are available for working it off through cycling or taking a hike southward at Port Hudson State Historic Site. A short ride away is the sister city of Jackson, a somewhat sleepy site, though packed with interesting history as it comprises ninety-six historical structures. It's a bit off the beaten path and geared for relaxing, antiquing and exploring early Louisiana history.

The Old Centenary Inn, a fetching bed-and-breakfast, is located downtown. It was built as a hotel in 1935 and assembled from materials recycled from a dormitory building of Jackson's Centenary College, founded in 1825. The charming accommodation has eight antique-filled rooms. A small self-operated elevator like the old days transports guests down to a sumptuous breakfast arranged in an elegant dining area. Jackson was the seat of Feliciana Parish until 1824, when the area was divided into East and West Feliciana Parishes. There was a need for lodging in Jackson in the early 1930s for visitors coming in to celebrate college graduations. Also, out-of-town doctors were called in to consult on patients at the local State Insane Asylum, which opened in 1848.

FREMIN'S RESTAURANT

402 West Third Street • Thibodaux, LA

Founded in the cypress-lined bend of Bayou Lafourche in 1830, the town of Thibodaux served as a trading post between New Orleans and the Bayou Teche country. The town flourished in the midst of sugar cane fields. Even today, it's common to follow a convoy of overloaded sugar cane trucks en route to the sugar mill. Originally known as Thibodeauxville, the town was settled by French and Spanish Creoles from New Orleans along with an influx of Acadian refugees.

This college town, as Nicholls State University is located here, retains its small-town charm with a scattering of bayous and swamps enticing fishermen as they haul their boats to the best secret fishing spots in Lafourche Parish.

The downtown, noted for its architecture, lends itself to exploring. This is the backdrop for law offices, the courthouse, nightlife spots, a sixty-year-old music store and the Wetlands Acadian Cultural Center, where you can drop in for a zydeco music jam on Monday nights.

A shining star of the historic downtown district is Fremin's Restaurant, set in a romantic setting reminiscent of New Orleans and located a stone's throw from Bayou Lafourche. The grand entrance of twin French doors is dazzling. Take in the grandeur of a rich mahogany bar, pressed tin ceilings, porcelain mosaic tile flooring and rich tapestries on the brick walls. A couple of dining tables are set near the beveled glass windows—during a golden era, patrons watched horse-drawn carriages ride by on dirt roads.

Built in 1878, the three-storied building of the eatery, originally known as the Roth Drugstore, has a wraparound wrought-iron balcony. It once accommodated a drugstore on the first floor, a laboratory and doctors' offices. Along with dispensing medicine, the drugstore had a soda fountain, drawing customers in from the hot day to enjoy an ice cream cone before heading to the Grand Theater around the corner. The third floor was used for living quarters, though it was heavily damaged in 1965 when Hurricane Betsy came calling.

In 1998, the local Fremin brothers—Dale, Francis and Barry—purchased the building, restoring it to its original show-off glory. The first floor now houses a bar, kitchen and dining area of the eatery. The second floor features original longleaf pine floors and beaded board walls and is used for private parties and ticketed special events during the holiday season, musical comedies and Bastille Weekend celebration.

The heritage of Lafourche Parish and the promotion of the Cajun Food Trail hails Thibodaux as a destination that packs a punch of festivals, unique eateries and scenic drives. Downtown events such as Mardi Gras, community art walks and the summertime Boogie on the Bayou Festival make Fremin's an ideal location to enjoy small bites, cocktails, or dessert.

Chef Kevin Templet, from the neighboring town of Labadieville, was ushered into Cajun and Creole dishes through an uncle who owned a grocery

The three-storied Fremin's Restaurant in Thibodaux was built in 1878 and offers fine dining in a dazzling atmosphere. *Courtesy of Fremin's Restaurant.*

store. Family members also shared their love of cooking. At age eleven, Kevin developed a recipe and technique of cooking when he competed in a barbecue cook-off for 4H—his special dish included chicken. He placed second and vowed to perfect his cooking abilities. Years later, he participated hands-on in a communal pig boucherie. Up at dawn, he worked with other chefs to prepare numerous dishes that come from traditional pig butchering.

Although he originally pursued an education in computer science, he was convinced to switch to a career in culinary arts though he never had any formal training, except through the school of hard knocks. This is where he experienced on-the-job training. He delved into cookbooks to hone his culinary techniques. Through trial and error, he was determined to learn from master chefs, gradually finding the Fremin family at Flanagan's Restaurant, where he signed on as sous chef. Open for lunch and dinner, Fremin's features Creole and Italian dishes as well as lighter fare such as soup, salad and sandwiches.

The signature pork dish at Fremin's is Abbeville Pork, a frenched center-cut pork loin chop set on a bed of andouille cornbread dressing topped with a cane syrup glaze and sided with fried sweet potatoes. Other dishes include smoked duck and andouille gumbo, Angus filet mignon, roasted rack of lamb, huge scallops devilishly prepared with magic sauces and rib-eye steak. A surprising appetizer is the sweet pork belly: braised pork belly with cane syrup, sweet potato puree, arugula salad and pickled turnips.

Chef Templet recalls one of the highlights of his career at Fremin's was when he received a special request from "Mac Rebennack" to prepare a special dinner. But you know "Mac" as the late New Orleans pianist and singer-songwriter Dr. John, and the requested dish was smothered rabbit.

Another honor occurred when Lafourche Parish was used as the setting for filming of the 2012 movie *Looper* 12 starring actors Bruce Willis and Emily Blunt. The movie crew of 150 were introduced to first-class cuisine at Fremin's Restaurant, which hosted a party to wow the movie crew.

HEBERT'S SPECIALTY MEATS

8212 US-167 • MAURICE, LA
(ADDITIONAL LOUISIANA LOCATIONS IN BATON ROUGE, BROUSSARD, LAKE CHARLES AND PRAIRIEVILLE)

It's a much-loved Cajun-style butcher shop acclaimed as "home of the Turducken." The original location of Hebert's (pronounced A-Bears) is in Vermilion Parish, with other franchise locations in Houston, Texas, and Destin, Florida. Since brothers Widley "Junior" and Sammy opened the original location of this friendly specialty meat market in 1984, a variety of boudin and Cajun favorites have been served. There are two ways to get your Cajun food cravings satisfied: through packaged meats in the coolers or prepared plate lunches of rice and gravy, pork roast or meatball stew.

A delightful array of stuffings are used in Hebert's renowned chicken. For something tame, there is cornbread or rice dressing. Take it up a notch with crawfish etouffee dressing or the alligator dressing that's packed into the deboned chicken, making for a delicious taste. A plate lunch of jambalaya is on the menu every Sunday. A long list of meat products is posted, featuring such delights as rabbit, Cornish hens, stuffed beef tongue or pork chops stuffed with fresh pork sausage and a special pepper jelly. It will make your head spin to decide what to slap on the counter for checkout.

Accolades point to this spot in Maurice, Louisiana, as the location where the original Turducken, the true epitome of "birds of a feather flock together," was created. The term comes from the combining of turkey, duck and chicken. The fractured name for this multi-fowl mix was added to recognized dictionaries in 2014. Basically, it's a bird within a bird, within another bird, all deboned and layered with dressing. Outside of the United States, the term for this unusual dish is a *three-bird roast*.

Preparing this big bird promises to be an arduous undertaking. It takes patience, practice and the right tools, though your first trial of three mixed-up birds may not be a pretty sight. Tools include skewers to hold the sections in place, a kitchen needle with a large eye and butcher's twine to stitch up the birds.

Hebert's version of the three poultry commingling is a culinary feat that stemmed from a 1984 visit from a local farmer who carried in a tub a chicken, duck and turkey he had just killed with the goal of cooking. He approached Hebert's owners Junior and Sammy with the odd request for assistance in combining the three plucked birds. He was in a real jam and needed help in creating a fabulous dish. The Heberts improvised with a hands-on approach of creative carving and filling the meaty jumble with cornbread dressing to compose an appealing entrée.

This beast of a bird includes choice parts, such as the white meat of a turkey and juicy meat of a chicken along with the wild taste of a duck. Hebert's version is padded with stuffing and liberally seasoned to weigh nearly twenty pounds. Its versatility is amazing, as the new bird can be roasted, braised, fried, grilled or barbecued. Marbled slices of this showstopper are served on Thanksgiving or Christmas. Hebert's staff is dedicated to their stations for the tasks of stuffing the lovely birds to the count of approximately two hundred a day. The legacy of the turducken has focused national media attention on the small shop with mentions in the *Wall Street Journal*, *New York Times*, the Travel Channel and the History Channel.

This imaginative dish represents a culinary process called engastration. This practice of stuffing and assembling the meat of one animal inside another dates to the Middle Ages. To flaunt their wealth and impress dinner guests, lords of the manor instructed their chefs to prepare a variety of meats, even going as far as creating an edible spectacle called cockentrice, which in today's standards may seem a little freakish. This combined the meat of a rooster and the head of a small pig. Stuffed with pork liver, nuts and fruit, the upper body of the pig was sewn, including the head, onto the bottom half of a plucked rooster and baked for hours.

Before the unusual turducken flew into the Hebert coop, the family started off in the food industry by introducing a restaurant in 1974 called Soop's—it closed in 2019. This served as the training ground where the Heberts learned how to debone and stuff chickens, cook alligator dressing and make crawfish pies. Endless other kitchen skills were taught by their father as a means of learning a trade. As the restaurant grew, the brothers saw an opportunity to specialize in specific products by opening a meat market.

From the time he was a tot, third-generation Sammy Hebert was ushered into the ins and outs of running a meat market. His experience includes every aspect of the shop, from prepping boudin to slicing and stuffing every type of meat that's housed to recommending cuts of meat to customers. Folks from far away may now enjoy all of the Cajun dishes. It's easy to share the "hot stuff," from pork roast to stuffed quail to alligator and pork mixed sausage, as everything is available for shipping.

HOT TAILS

1113 Hospital Road • New Roads, LA

The place reminds one of the phrase "country comes to town" with its barn-like style. Tin roofing, chicken coops, recycled old doors and chicken wire make up the décor of the comfy setting. The building originated as a drive-through convenience store that sold the "hot tails" of boiled crawfish. Husband and wife Cody and Samantha Carroll both graduated as chefs from the Louisiana Culinary Institute in Baton Rouge and reached for the stars. They set their sights on New Roads, one of the oldest settlements in the Mississippi Valley, to open a restaurant to dish up their own version of Cajun and Creole cuisine.

The menu showcases grilled dishes such as rib-eyes and filet mignon with distinctive toppings. Fried rabbit is paired with slow-cooked red beans. A Southern fried pork chop, sprinkled with Cajun seasoning, is sandwiched between two slices of Texas toast. Starters feature precious Louisiana crustaceans like crawfish bread, which is a hollowed-out French bread loaf brimming with spinach and artichoke dip and topped with fried crawfish tails. Their take on buffalo wings is one-of-a-kind with crispy duck drumettes that are drizzled with pepper jelly and remoulade sauce.

Home grown and adventurous, the Carrolls recently starred in the Food Network series *Cajun Aces* which followed the couple through fishing and hunting exploits plus the juggling act of managing a restaurant. Hot Tails will open a second location in Prairieville, Louisiana, in 2020.

JOHNSON'S BOUCANIERE

1111 St. John Street • Lafayette, LA

Sitting on the wraparound porch downtown at the Boucaniere is about as good as it gets. Take in the sounds of church bells ringing from St. John's Cathedral down the street. A whiff from the smokehouse behind the store tempts you to order a heaping helping of good eats through rain or shine. If the timing is right, you may also enjoy conversations with the Johnsons, who have been serving boudin and other meats since 1937.

The family hails from Eunice, the prairie Cajun capital of Louisiana. Rice farms were a common sight in the region, as the staple of rice stars as an essential ingredient for Cajun dishes such as gumbo, jambalaya and rice and gravy. At Johnson's shop, boudin, the snack/meal you love to squeeze, takes center stage.

When Arneastor Johnson opened up a shoebox-sized grocery store in Eunice in 1939, the setup was simple. The wooden floor and shelves from ceiling to floor were filled with a variety of dry staples. He sold live chickens and whatever else his customers needed. Rather than cooling off with an air conditioner during the hot days of summer, big fans were set up to get the air circulating.

Oak wood was used in the backyard smokehouse built of cinderblock. Well-versed in the task of preparing boudin through family boucheries, the Johnsons began making and selling their own boudin at the store until it closed in 2005, mostly

Lori Johnson Walls starts her day with making meaty boudin links. *Courtesy of Johnson's Boucaniere.*

Doris Johnson cooking a endless supply of rice, getting ready to make boudin. *Courtesy of Johnson's Boucaniere.*

due to competition from supermarkets. Arneastor's five children worked in the store, including Wallace Johnson, who is now in his nineties.

A revival of the Johnsons' expertise occurred in 2008 when Arneastor's granddaughter Lori Johnson Walls and her husband, architect Greg Walls, opened Johnson's Boucaniere in downtown Lafayette (*boucaniere* is French for "smokehouse"). Lori's father, Wallace, keeps a watchful eye and shares family recipes and techniques of making a memorable link of boudin, sausage and other smoked meats.

A bit of a self-proclaimed rascal, Wallace recalls early days at the family grocery store. An early assignment was sweeping the wooden floor with used motor oil to keep the dust down. As he was promoted up the corporate ladder of the meat market, he took orders from customers. He also progressed to cleaning the skin off onions and stacking them neatly in a bin. Eventually he became the manager of the humble grocery store. There was no cash register, so a cigar box was used to store money from sales that were tallied daily. No music played in the store because they didn't have a spare radio. There was a lot of spirited conversation, mostly in French. Beer was not sold in the store because applying for a liquor license was expensive. Countless links of boudin changed hands; their best day was a quantity of two thousand links of boudin sold before lunchtime. The serving line for boudin streamed out the door into the parking lot. The phone rang off the wall with call-in orders coming through.

Wallace served as backup butcher for cutting pork chops and prepping to fry cracklings. The store was closed on Sundays. Groceries were delivered by a horse-drawn wagon to neighborhood customers. The horse was named Dempsey after boxer Jack Dempsey. The delivery mode transitioned to bicycling during World War II, as gas was rationed. Wallace carefully transported staples such as eggs and beans in a basket.

He recalls the tradition of the country boucherie, which was always held on Saturdays during wintertime because there was no refrigeration to store the meat once the pig was slaughtered. As a boy, Wallace was given responsibility by his elders and helped with the butchering by opening up the pig, removing the intestines, rubbing it with baking soda and cleaning it inside and out. The boucherie was an all-day affair and an exciting social event he looked forward to, as it gave him playtime with his cousins.

And what is Wallace's job at Johnson's Boucaniere today? He's good at spinning old records on the record player. He scribbles customers' orders as well, and he entertains with humorous stories. Although he and his siblings worked hard in the store, it was nothing compared to the backbreaking hours when his family worked what his father referred to as a "cotton patch," which was actually acres and acres of cotton fields. As an adolescent, Wallace spent many days picking cotton. The season usually included visiting the same cotton rows numerous times, bending over and plucking the cotton bolls off the stems. The process seemed never-ending through many seasons.

During his high school years, he participated in a boxing team, which led to a short career as a professional featherweight boxer. He won one boxing match and proudly added "Undefeated Professional Boxer" to his list of accolades. He is also an accomplished artist, with many of his folk-style oil paintings adorning the store walls.

After the shop's lunch rush, customers drop by from either down the street or from across the country. Word of mouth proclaims this as a "must eat" in Lafayette. Wallace enjoys taking a break by enjoying a bite of dessert like the homemade "hello dollies" sweets that are on hand as he grabs a cup of coffee. He reminisces about the old store and has an amazing memory. The original meat market building that his father opened still stands in Eunice. Some of the artifacts from the old place have been recycled and made their way to the Lafayette store—like the large enamel scale that was used to weigh meat, with a pricing sheet intact from the early days, a pie safe (called a *garde manger* or "keeper of the food") and a wooden bread slicer his grandfather Hypolite Gaspard built during the 1940s when there was a metal shortage due to World War II.

Today, Lori Johnson Walls, tagged as the sausage-maker's daughter, with her husband, Greg Walls, an architect by profession who designed the restaurant, have taken over the helm. They make boudin and work hands-on to cook Cajun plate lunches for their customers. They serve a boucaniere breakfast bowl of biscuits topped with a fried egg. Other eatables include a stuffed grilled cheese biscuit with boudin or grits topped with a splattering of pulled pork. The boudin, made from a blend of cooked rice, Boston butt pork and liver with onions, bell pepper and cayenne seasoning, draws visitors from the many festivals Lafayette hosts. Johnson's Boucaniere flagship event is the Boudin Cook-Off held every October in downtown Lafayette. The Walls have received the "Un-Link Specialty Award" for their pork belly sliders, a quirky combo of pork belly, boudin balls and aioli. Johnson's Boucaniere menu runs the gamut from favorite Cajun dishes like chicken and sausage gumbo (their in-house smoked sausage is added) to a smoked meat poboy or a smoked meat salad. Feel free to lick your fingers for the slow-smoked country-style barbecue ribs.

LAURA'S II

1904 WEST UNIVERSITY AVENUE • LAFAYETTE, LA

Madonna Broussard inherited the laurels as "Plate Lunch Queen" from her grandmother Laura Williams Broussard, the namesake of the acclaimed Creole restaurant called Laura's II.

Born in 1920, Grandmother Laura was considered a "city girl," as she lived near downtown within the big city of Lafayette. French was her first language, and she attended school for only a few years, instead tasked with staying home to cook for her siblings and helping to raise the family while her parents worked. When Laura was grown, she gained experience by cooking in a downtown Lafayette club called Sam's Star Lounge.

In a gutsy move, she opened an underground kitchen in her own home in the 1960s to make a living. While the front of the house was set up to feed neighborhood customers, the rear of the house accommodated her family. At one time, proprietors of restaurants or shops often lived atop or adjacent to their businesses as a convenience for the owner to be only a few steps away from their establishment's front door.

For Laura's venture, slow-cooked pork roast or other Creole dishes simmered on the stove by dawn, making this one of the first soul food plate lunch spots in Lafayette. To draw customers in on Wednesdays, she offered stuffed baked turkey wings to rave reviews with just the right snippets of garlic and spices and a liberal sprinkling of cayenne. In addition to cooking hefty meals, she bought pounds of pork pieces, did all the grinding and spent all day making boudin, including blood boudin for her customers.

Despite a devastating fire in the restaurant/house in the 1970s, Laura relocated to a metal building at a dead-end street in a residential neighborhood until she retired in 1984. Laura's son Harold and daughter-in-law Dorothy Phillips Broussard, Madonna's mother, took over cooking duties through the years. Catering to customers came naturally to "Dot" as she served smothered pork chops or gumbo. She enjoyed pampering her customers by throwing out some terms of endearment like *cher* and *baby* in appreciation. By upgrading the menu, more country cooking dishes like pork shank stew and pig's feet became favorites.

In 2000, the restaurant moved to its current site, convenient to downtown, college campuses and main thoroughfares. This is when third-generation kitchen wizard Madonna Broussard took over in the kitchen. No stranger to rice and gravy, she considers herself a country girl, having been raised on a farm in Parks, Louisiana. She is familiar with the term *farm-to-table* and has been surrounded by the food industry all of her life, recalling the tasks of picking okra, sweet potatoes and corn from the fields along with preparing side dishes in the kitchen. Boucheries were traditions held every winter. "We had to eat everything they killed. This included the stomach, the tongue and hogshead cheese, although cracklings were usually the first dish that was ready for munching," she admitted.

Her future was certainly not written in stone, as she never envisioned that one day she would wear a company apron to join the family in the restaurant business. Instead, she worked for ten years at a Fruit of the Loom plant in St. Martinville. But today she proudly lives up to the nickname "Plate Lunch Queen" by following in the footsteps of her grandmother and mother. Laura had a big presence, as she was "traditionally built." No one doubted that she was the boss in the kitchen. She was well organized and knew where everything was located, how long to stir a dish, how much seasoning was needed, when to add more water and when the dish was ready for serving.

Laura's was closed on Sundays back in the day. After attending Mass, Laura spent hours preparing spreads of dishes for family, as it was a traditional get-together. Despite early hours and long days in the kitchen cooking for customers, Laura enjoyed creating a red carpet array of Sunday dinner for family members. Madonna remembers her grandmother's special dish of yams with pecans and marshmallow. Refusing to eat a dish was taboo, as you were expected to sample everything.

The eatery's name, Laura's II, was given to acknowledge that the current spot is the second location with its casual living room atmosphere. The Creole experience of chicken fricassee and homegrown smothered okra is enjoyed by folks from all walks of life—attorneys from downtown, students from local colleges, medical workers from nearby hospitals, cyclists riding by and visitors in town for festivals.

There's a lot of finger-licking going on in the eatery. Many fans are hooked on Laura's rice and gravy and memorize which day of the week has their favorite dish on the serving line. Red beans and rice is cooked on Monday. The comfort food of chicken and sausage gumbo is served on crisp winter days. And usually a seafood dish like shrimp stew or fried catfish is prepared on Fridays, especially during Lent. Every day fried chicken, fried pork chops and stuffed baked turkey wings from Laura's original recipes are served. Barbeque chicken and ribs covered with a devilish sweet and tangy barbecue sauce are lined up on Thursdays and Sundays.

Brawny turkey wings, sinfully seasoned and baked, begin as a three-jointed turkey wing. The one hundred or so turkey wings that are prepared daily are stuffed with garlic and pepper and oven baked in metal pans for hours until crispy on the outside though juicy inside.

The menu items are considered soul food, a term popularized in the South during the 1960s. The culinary style derived from the recipes, methods of cooking and seasoning perfected by the African American community includes an unlimited number of pork dishes—pigs' feet, ham hocks, ears, hog jowl and chitlings. These pig parts also add flavoring to slowly cooked greens or beans.

A festival called Plate Lunch A-Palooza is held every September in the Sugar Mill Pond area of Lafayette and is presented by spice mogul Tony Chachere. Chefs from restaurants and catering businesses join together to prepare comfort food. And the red carpet is spread for Madonna to prepare a meatball stew sided with green beans.

The Creole eatery received national acclaim in 2018 when celebrity chef Anthony Bourdain dropped in to enjoy lunch as he filmed one of his final episodes of *Parts Unknown*, a CNN show that explores cultures and cuisine. The timeframe was Mardi Gras week, and in the midst of prepping her dishes, Madonna was given fifteen minutes' notice by local musician Sid Williams that Bourdain was hungry and planned to stop by to sample her Creole dishes. Not only was Bourdain going to have lunch, but he was going to include her and the eatery in his popular show. Once Bourdain and his crew arrived, the restaurant was magically transformed into a TV set.

Another generation follows in the footsteps of matriarch Laura by taking over as dishes sizzle at the stove. Madonna's children have both been involved in the restaurant, starting with tasks such as busing the tables and learning how to cook Laura's best-loved dishes.

MOWATA STORE

30283 Crowley Eunice Highway (Hwy 13) • Mowata, LA

The community of Mowata in Acadia Parish may not be pinpointed on all road maps. But it's worth the jaunt along the Cajun prairie lands among rice fields and crawfish ponds. The area shares German as well as a Cajun heritage. Although many guess that the name is derived from a Native

American word, that's not the case. Rather, as trains used to run through the area as a rail stop, a sign to identify the area along with the need for "More Water," the signage was mistakenly printed as "Mowata."

With more than twenty-five years' experience of making boudin and smoking meats, owner Bubba Frey of the Mowata Store is also a master accordion player.

The store is woodsy all the way, from the front porch, which has seating, to the hardwood flooring, walls and ceiling. Aside from the juicy boudin, cracklings, turkey wings and bacon-wrapped pork-stuffed jalapeño peppers, there's an interesting array of other items. The on-site smokehouse is stocked with sausage and other delectables. Mowata's has farm-raised fresh eggs, a stash of turkeys on his farm Frey will smoke for holidays, pickled quail eggs, muscadine jelly, chow chow and hog lard roux, made with flour and rendered pork fat.

NONC KEV'S

1421 The Boulevard • Rayne, LA

If you have the heart of a Cajun and love the culture and off-the-wall dishes, you'll fit in. When Houston-bred Kevin Underwood moved to the Acadia Parish community of Mire when he was a teenager, he embraced the culture. During high school, he worked part-time in a local grocery store as a bag boy. When an opportunity arose to work in the meat market section, he jumped at the chance.

Through his sixteen years there and eventual promotion to manager, he learned the culinary arts of how to cut beef, chicken and pork; how to recognize the difference between a rump roast and loin; and how to conduct an eagle-eyed inspection.

Kevin and his wife, Crystal, were encouraged to open their own business, and they agreed that a specialty meat store in a smaller town would be ideal. That was in 2017, and Nonc Kev's opened right off I-10 in Rayne. Considering that he was a crackerjack at making boudin and other Cajun dishes and was fortunate enough to be someone's uncle, he tagged the business Nonc Kev's, as *nonc* is an abbreviation for the French word for uncle. Crystal has memories of her annual Forestier family boucheries and vividly recalls the cutting up of the pig and preparation of numerous dishes to share.

A Cajun boucherie is a dawn to dusk celebration. *Courtesy of Annette Huval.*

The shop has a friendly name, and for a small setup and great location, it's an unpretentious spot to pick up grub through the drive-through window. The store opens at 5:30 a.m. on weekdays. Plate lunches are available Monday through Friday with local favorites like pork and sausage jambalaya or mini pork roast rice and gravy, all with two side dishes. The kitchen also offers burgers, tasso sandwiches, boudin (regular and a spicier smoked boudin that has a little crunch to it), golf ball–sized batter-fried boudin balls and cracklings.

Nonc Kev's created its own seasoning and barbecue sauce, which made it easier to pick up a variety of meats. Check the display for rib-eyes, stuffed beef tongue, alligator nuggets, marinated rabbit, boneless chicken breasts stuffed with crawfish boudin and pork chops to tote home to cook for you name it—tailgating at the football game or a graduation event. Appetizers like bacon-wrapped asparagus and crab-stuffed mushrooms are also plentiful on the shelf. Holidays mean turkey rolls and pork roasts.

Unique appetizers come with a promise to fill you up. The Boudin Biscuit is a lofty homemade biscuit that is slammed with a boudin patty that has been deep fried and drizzled with the Louisiana sweetener of Steen's cane syrup.

There's an Asian influence in the Steen Syrup Boudin Rollup. The boudin meat mixture of cooked ground pork and rice is combined with the right proportion of cane syrup. Then a big spoonful of the mixture is added to an egg roll wrapper, which is then deep fried.

You can also fuel up your car at the shop. But it can get busy during festival time; folks are drawn to the somewhat unusual famous frog jumping contest in May at the Rayne Frog Festival and the K-Bon Radio Station 101.1 Music Festival in October.

NORBERT'S RESTAURANT

521 Avenue C, Highway 90 East • Broussard, LA

John Norbert grew up in Broussard in a household with a big group at the dinner table. His father and grandfather raised cows and pigs, and pig boucheries or cochon de laits were held annually in the winter. A beef boucherie in which cows were slaughtered was also hosted by the Norbert family every summer.

John has many years of experience as a butcher in local meat markets, and he has the leather-like hands to prove it. He and his wife, Lille Mae, enjoyed cooking for family get-togethers and were encouraged to open their own restaurant. In 1970, they opened an eatery on Morgan Street, near the only traffic light at the time in downtown Broussard. The building was a plain shuttered grocery store. After a few years of growing success at the stove, they expanded to their current location along Highway 90. It may be kismet, as this spot happens to be directly across from where John grew up.

They dedicated long hours to hard work, arriving at the eatery at 3:00 a.m. for a cycle of serving breakfast, cleaning up, cooking lunch and cleaning up once again. Then it was time to cook dinner, clean up one more time, and shut the doors at 11:00 p.m. This routine took place seven days a week. Though the time on their feet proved demanding, they embraced friendly banter with customers as they perfected the art of home-style cooking. The couple love what they do, and at one time, their commitment paid for college for their two daughters: Jolene is a dietician in Houston and Millicent an events coordinator at Vermilionville in Lafayette. Once their daughters' education needs were met, the Norberts scaled back, though they continue to make boudin and fry cracklings and cook some of the greatest plate lunches in the region. Hand-sized pork/beef meat pies can be ordered ahead of time

John Norbert is experienced in cooking many Cajun favorites. *Courtesy of Annette Huval.*

for easy pickup. Sweet potato pie with crimped crust is lovingly prepared by Lille Mae as the pleasing end to a good meal.

Norbert's is a true landmark that's a couple of notches above the norm for Cajun cuisine. It's considered Broussard's oldest sit-down eatery. A crazy quilt of black-and-white pictures of the old downtown hangs on the wall along with a signed poster of local zydeco musical legend and valued Norbert's customer Geno Delafose.

It's the talk of the town for heart-warming dishes. The parade of plate lunches posted on the chalkboard varies on weekdays to include smothered rabbit and red beans and rice on Mondays. Thursdays are for saucy, slow-cooked barbecued ribs. Scoops of thick and meaty rice and gravy are served every weekday. The practice of a Cajun plate lunch stems from farming days when the main meal was lunch to help sustain long days in the field. It usually included a meat that had been slow cooked since dawn, rice and gravy, a side of beans or a stewed vegetable and a slice of bread.

To reach others and share the cuisine with the younger generation, the Norberts cook their pork jambalaya for Lafayette's springtime Festivals International.

Always with a mischievous grin on his face, John is a young eighty-six. What keeps him youthful is the enjoyment of adding a generous touch of cayenne pepper to his dishes, joking around with his customers and his love for keeping active, such as zydeco dancing. Cooking is one of his passions, although he is open to mastering the keys of an accordion; it's on his bucket list.

OLD COURTABLEAU CAFÉ

104 SOUTH MAIN STREET • WASHINGTON, LA

As a leading center of commerce in the 1800s, the winsome town of Washington ruled the waters as the largest inland port between New Orleans and St. Louis, Missouri. At one time, Washington's town squares included a cotton gin, a cottonseed oil mill, a distinguished opera house, a shop specializing in making buggies, a cooper shop for making barrels and a stagecoach line station. Floating stores of merchandise used Washington as a takeoff point. These stores on boats carried medicine, spices and necessities. Merchants stopped at every port to sell their wares.

Workers scurried to load and unload cargo from steamboats, barges and wagons. The dockside was alive with trade activities. Cotton and other crops from nearby plantations were delivered to Washington on flatboats. They were stored in warehouses that lined the bayou and readied for shipments to New Orleans. Riches of wine, whiskey, cigars, coffee beans, silk, champagne, fine china and exotic food supplies were imported from Europe and Cuba.

The town continues to reflect a passion for its history. Listed in the National Register of Historic Places since 1978, 80 percent of Washington's buildings have been identified as being of historic significance. One of the factors affecting major change in this steamboat town was the arrival of the railroad in the late 1800s, which diminished river traffic. The Civil War also changed the dynamics of Washington's role as a leading inland port. With Union occupation of the area, engineers cut off waterways, limiting transportation to and from New Orleans.

Visitors hunting for collectibles veer off Interstate 49 to shop at the Old Schoolhouse Antique Mall in Washington, a superstore of booths. They feature vintage tools, houseware, jewelry and virtually everything from the "old days." The town's public library, museum and bed-and-breakfasts are all housed in noteworthy buildings and houses. An annual Catfish Festival honors the whiskered freshwater delight, which can be cooked, fried or grilled. The town is considered Louisiana's third-oldest settlement and will celebrate its tricentennial in 2020.

For over twenty years, the team of David and Peggy Allemond operated a popular dancehall/café/swamp tour business thirty miles away in Henderson, Louisiana. It was situated along the levee overlooking the Atchafalaya Basin, and they lived in a houseboat. Memories linger from Sunday afternoons of enjoying a lunchtime poboy followed by hours of stomping to Cajun music at McGee's. This area played an integral part of David's roots, as he enjoyed the outdoors: dropping a line to catch catfish, boating alongside alligators and hunting deer. Allemond's Cajun Tom Sawyer childhood took place in the Atchafalaya Basin, America's largest wetland swamp, known for its unique sunsets, bounty of wildlife and ancient cypress trees.

In 2016, the family opted to sell McGee's to a Boy Scout organization that turned the property into an educational center. But retirement did not last long, as the Allemonds pursued another opportunity, this time in Washington, Louisiana, where David's great-grandfather, a physician, once lived. There was an available 1820s building located in an appealing neighborhood of Washington. The building had lived many lives as a general mercantile, a drugstore, a meat market and a hardware store.

Though built to last, the structure needed refurbishing. Rustic metal and wood planks make up the skeleton of the interior. Much of the country décor was salvaged from the old McGee's in Henderson and reused to update the Old Courtableau Café to transform it with a homespun appeal. Considering the number of patrons who have walked the floors through the lifespan of the place, the wooden floors retain creaks and slight dips, which add to the character of the café.

The wide-open atmosphere has wooden booths, passé partouts (old saws) displayed and a bandstand named in honor of Cajun fiddler, guitarist and family friend Al Berard, who passed away in 2014. The remodeling of the building took a year of rewiring and enlarging the kitchen. New additions included a cypress bar that was inherited from the Allemonds' former business. The appeal of selecting Washington as their next adventure began with research that David's great-grandfather was a doctor in Washington. The café building was dedicated to honor David's mother, the late Geraldine Robin.

A humdinger of a menu includes steaks and seafood with favorites such as crab cakes, poboys and a variety of grilled and smothered dishes. "We got your rice and gravy," is one of the cook's mottos. The crawfish maque choux egg roll is a one-of-a-kind appetizer with a smoky taste derived from the tasso, a key ingredient of the dish. Boiled crawfish is served seasonally, directly from the family's fifty-two-acre crawfish farm. Barbecue ribs, pork and chicken are available on Sundays for lunch. Freshly baked desserts are displayed daily. Come dressed up or in jeans to enjoy live music performed on weekends. The old-fashioned juke box shares Cajun favorites during weekdays.

As an extra touch, there are some special guests—ghosts roaming through—as staff have reported unexplained shadows and flashes of light. There are several old cemeteries nearby; one dates to 1700, which offers history buffs a reason to stop off the beaten path in Washington.

PAP'S SAUSAGE KITCHEN

Swords Community • 244 Severan Road • Church Point, LA

It's truly a mom-and-pop kitchen located in an area called Swords, located down a dead-end gravel road where chickens waltz freely in the neighborhood. Racks of sausage, ribs and other pig parts fill the two cinderblock smokehouses, stacked with red oak and pecan wood. The storefront is located behind Bertman "Pap" and Charlene Papillion's brick house. Word of mouth is usually what attracts folks to this country store, which carries an assortment of Cajun delights.

There's andouille and a well-seasoned tasso to throw into your gumbo, rice dressing mix, old-time big boulettes (meatballs), smoked stuffed ponce (pig stomach), slab bacon and an assortment of other meats. In the wintertime, the Papillions stay busy by processing deer meat from hunters. Aside from walk-in customers who recognize Pap's sign at the front of the road off Highway 190, there are regular customers in Houston, Denver and Alaska who are reminded of home every time they receive the choice food product shipments.

The tasks of making boudin and sausage have been modernized and simplified from earlier days. While the original cast-iron sausage stuffer had a hand crank, the tools have been upgraded. A hydraulic sausage stuffer is used, and it requires only one person to handle the tasks. The boudin casing slides onto the nozzle of the sausage stuffer to guide the mix of cooked rice, pork, vegetables and seasoning through the machinery to prepare meaty links of boudin.

The Papillions are well-versed in the tradition of family boucheries in which chores were assigned to every family member to help in the pig slaughter of hogs. It was from this experience that the Papillions learned how to make the many dishes derived from pork.

RITA MAE'S KITCHEN

711 Federal Avenue • Morgan City, LA

Tigre Island, Brashear City, "Gateway to the Atchafalaya" and "Jumbo Shrimp Capital of the World" are many names for Morgan City, Louisiana. The city blends several heritages—namely, French, Spanish, Italian, German, Dutch, Native American and African American—in its diverse influences.

The area was known as Tigre Island when a group of U.S. surveyors spotted a large, mysterious cat nearby. The region also attracted the attention of Kentucky planter and surgeon Walter Brashear. Brashear's subsequent subdividing of his sugar cane plantation was the beginning of the first permanent settlement known as the town of Brashear.

Get spoiled at Rita Mae's Kitchen in Morgan City. *Author's collection.*

119

Located near the Atchafalaya River, Tigre Island was occupied by Federal troops for over three years during the Civil War due to its strategic marine location. The town grew after the war through a growth spurt of importing opportunities when steamship/railroad entrepreneur Charles Morgan oversaw dredging the Atchafalaya Bay Channel. The town was renamed in 1876 in honor of Charles Morgan. It became a trade center for cypress timber, seafood and other commodities.

During the early 1900s, the town continued to grow. Many historic buildings such as Sacred Heart Catholic Church, Trinity Episcopal Church and Pharr Chapel Methodist were constructed. Boat building, moss picking and a shell crushing plant broadened Morgan City's economic base.

In 1937, Morgan City became known as the jumbo shrimp capital of the world. A blessing of the fleet was held to ensure a safe return and a bountiful harvest. The town hosts an annual Louisiana Shrimp and Petroleum Festival.

In downtown Morgan City, get ready to be spoiled as you take a seat in a setting reminiscent of your grandma's. A cup of your favorite coffee is poured at Rita Mae's Kitchen, and you're set to begin your day. It's always sunshine over this brightly painted house turned café on a tree-shaded boulevard in a neighborhood of Victorian houses, churches and specialty shops.

Colorful geegaws are scattered in a homey aura. You'll get your gumbo and your plate lunch with smothered pork served within a vessel of rice and gravy and lima beans, all Southern-style comfort food.

Drivers heading east to New Orleans often opt to drive on Highway 90 instead of getting frustrated by the traffic jams on I-10. When your stomach is grumbling, veer off to Morgan City and let Rita Mae take care of you.

For breakfast, you can have it your way with strong, steaming coffee, grits, eggs, bacon and sausage patties. For lunch, there's your gumbo, and no jaws will drop if you add a scoop of the potato salad into your gumbo. To some, it may be considered an unusual combination, as gumbos are already served with a starch, namely rice. Hey, it's acceptable as a Cajun tradition to add potato salad!

Eight tables are scattered in the café, and a counter offers a line of stools in the glassed-in front porch. Pick your spot as you make new friends. It's all smiles as the rack of freshly baked biscuits comes out of the oven. For lunch, you have hamburgers, plenty of seafood choices, fried chicken and other Southern specialties. Queen Rita has been courting diners at her café for twenty-five years.

"THE SAUSAGE BREAD LADY"

JOAN KAISER BERGEAUX • KROTZ SPRINGS, LA

It's a story of family and tradition with some twists and turns.

When someone lives to celebrate their ninetieth birthday and is introduced to their first ever blood relative at the same time, it can be considered an auspicious occasion. During the celebration, Loretta Cole Kaiser of Krotz Springs, Louisiana, met her first blood relative outside of her fourteen biological children. She grew up, as her mother, Loretta Rose, did also, without knowing of her family history.

Through Loretta Cole Kaiser's daughter Joan Bergeaux and granddaughter Janel Simien an effort was initiated to research their mother's and grandmother's history through DNA testing and online resources. They spent hours tracking down a first cousin living in Los Angeles, California. Through further research, it was discovered that Loretta Rose was born in New York City and given up for adoption. A family group traveled to New York City to scout around and visit the New York Foundling Hospital in search of solving the mystery of their heritage.

Loretta Cole Kaiser's parents were Loretta Rose Rosenfeldt Deville Cole and William Frederick Cole. Both of her parents were orphan train riders who arrived at the Opelousas, Louisiana station in the early 1900s when William was four and Loretta was two. The children were among hundreds of others who were orphaned at a young age and transported west.

With a surge of hundreds of thousands of immigrants coming into the United States in the late 1800s and settling in New York City, overpopulation became a problem. Many homeless children lived on the streets; they were either orphans or their parents could not take care of them because of a lack of available jobs.

Charles Loring Brace, through the Children's Aid Society, created the orphan train concept as a humanitarian means to relocate orphans from the overcrowded streets of New York City to other states. Providing good homes, education and jobs for these children was the goal. The orphan train is considered the largest child migration in the United States; approximately 250,000 children, aged infant to teenager, were transported by train from New York City to pre-selected towns in forty-five states, including Louisiana.

The first orphan train traveled from Albany, New York, to the Midwest in 1854. One of the last orphan trains traveled to Sulphur Springs, Texas, in 1929. Announcements were made throughout the United States, through posters at general stores or through church services. Louisiana received two thousand children via the orphan train. The children, some of whom did not speak English, were dressed in a new set of clothes, pinned with a number tag to identify them and given a Bible. Once arriving to one of the designated train stops, they were guided to a train platform for families to scrutinize them. Some children were preassigned before arrival, though some were taken away "on the spot."

Prospective parents often requested a certain type of child, preferring a specific characteristic such as gender, hair color or age. One of the stops was in the French-Louisiana town of Opelousas, the stop from which Loretta Rose and Willie Cole both descended. They were lined up in front of crowds of curious onlookers and adopted by families. Although many of these children were legally adopted by their new families, some remained indentured and worked for their room and board.

Loretta Rose's biological mother, Perle Wichard Rosenfeldt Stern, a native of Minsk, Russia, landed at Ellis Island in 1904 at age fourteen. She was reunited with an older sister who had immigrated to America a few years earlier. Some immigrants relied on a process called chain migration, whereby a family member would move to America to find appropriate accommodations. They found jobs and saved up money to send funds back to their homeland to loved ones so they could be reunited in America the land of opportunity. Many eastern European Jews came to America fleeing both economic hardship and violence.

At age fourteen, Perle, who later became a seamstress by trade, bore a baby out of wedlock and gave up the baby for adoption. The baby, Loretta Rose, was baptized and carried over to the New York Foundling Hospital to be raised by the Sisters of Charity, a Catholic organization. At age two, Loretta Rose became a rider on the orphan train.

Loretta Rose Cole died at a young age due to illness. Her daughter, Loretta Cole Kaiser, was only two years old when her mother died. Her brother, Arthur, was killed during his tour of duty in World War II while he was stationed in New Guinea. Loretta Cole married Claude Kaiser and had fifteen children, including an adopted baby girl from Vietnam.

As busy as she was with her large brood underfoot, Loretta Kaiser became known as the "Sausage Bread Lady" through a home business. Throughout her married life, she enjoyed working in the kitchen and preparing stuffed sausage bread for customers. Many years earlier, a family member from Melville, Louisiana, introduced Loretta to homemade sausage bread that charmed everyone as a savory delight. With such a big family to feed, Loretta used the same family recipe and improvised it to a simpler, more economical version with ground beef as well as pork sausage.

Loretta shared the family recipe, along with her love of baking and cooking with her daughter, so now Joan has taken over kneading the dough. The bread is made and sold at the Cajun Corner Café in Krotz Springs. To draw more customers in, Joan created a boudin ball recipe and started stuffing the bread with the unique mixture along with pepper jack cheese. And it's topped with crackling crumbs, so the dish is similar to a boudin king cake. Through every step of bread making, she reflects on her mother and the journey of her grandparents.

SOILEAU'S DINNER CLUB

1618 North Main Street • Opelousas, LA

With the first hint of cool weather coming through, cooks rush to prepare gumbo. Buy roux in a jar or the ingredients to make your own. Pick up andouille, onions, bell peppers, celery, chicken and rice. If you have a hankering to treat yourself to the next best thing, try a Cajun restaurant that offers true home cooking.

Soileau's (pronounced swallows) Dinner Club is a no-frills eatery, decorated in a '70s theme with interior brick walls, small windows and a gigantic stuffed fish hanging on the walls. Keep in mind the pronunciation. If you say "Soileau's" otherwise, it will be understood that you're not from Cajun country.

Let's brag about the food, as it is reasonably priced; service is good, and the atmosphere includes low-key, muted lighting. The menu is impressive. The eatery is tagged as a dinner club, but Soileau's is also open for luncheon specials. Steak and seafood are favorites. The cooks also offer hen and sausage gumbo. As many Cajuns brag, the best gumbo to cook on cold winter days is an "old tough hen" thrown into the gumbo pot and left to simmer on the stove for hours. Center-cut pork chops are also popular, as are poboys with a generous serving of shrimp. One of Soileau's signature dishes is the Southern fried chicken, y'all.

The restaurant is located on a main thoroughfare in Opelousas. Soileau's opened in 1937, when Main Street was a dirt road. Clarence Soileau rented a gas station on Washington Road north Opelousas. He ripped out gas pumps to make room for setting up tables and chairs. Voilà—Soileau's Place was opened for business. At the time, cooks and owners Clarence and his wife, Mable, focused on thirty-five-cent plate lunches by selling barbecue chicken halves right off the pit with trimmings. As the number of customers grew, the popular Soileau's Place transitioned to Soileau's Dinner Club, with Clarence and his brother-in-law Cliff Veillon heading up the business. The restaurant closed briefly in 1942 during wartime when Clarence served his country by moving to New Orleans to work in the shipyards.

The eatery remains family run, now overseen by third-generation Soileaus. The legacy continues, even through hardships. The Great Depression stilted the local economy and affected customers' budgets. A fire destroyed the restaurant in 1966, though it was rebuilt a few blocks away to reopen within a few months.

Recognized as ambassadors of tourism, the Soileaus have been honored through the Louisiana Restaurant Association. Second-generation restaurateur Scott Soileau and wife, Beth Deville Soileau, were named 2017 Restaurateur of the Year. During the same year, they were inducted into Louisiana Restaurant Hall of Fame.

SPILLWAY CAFÉ

599 Morganza Highway • Morganza, LA

Rev up your car to take a ride to this unassuming village with a couple of surprises. It's divided by two main streets with a railroad track in the middle. Morganza was established in 1908 in honor of Colonel Charles Morgan, the first American sheriff of Pointe Coupee Parish and developer of Morganza Plantation. The site of a Civil War battle, the town was once thriving and populated with several shops operated by Italian entrepreneurs.

Revitalization efforts are underway to draw visitors to this region, which has many claims to fame, including an important chapter in Louisiana's coastal story that continues today. The Morganza Spillway is a U.S. Army Corps of Engineers flood-control structure with locks and levees designed to divert water from the Mississippi River. It was critical to design a solution for major flooding following the Great Flood of 1927. The spillway was completed in 1954.

Strike a nostalgic chord to reconnect to the past: Morganza sites were used as scenes in the cult classic and award-winning *Easy Rider* in 1969. Hollywood stars Peter Fonda, Dennis Hopper and newcomer Jack Nicholson dropped by to get a view of small-town USA Louisiana style, complete with all of its unique cuisine. In the movie, the plot follows free-spirited, long-haired bikers dining in a fictitious restaurant named Melancon's and camping out near the Morganza Spillway. You can't underplay the importance of the publicity that came from being the center of attention for a movie that won eight of fourteen Academy Award nominations.

To commemorate the fiftieth anniversary of the movie, a huge celebration was held in September 2019. Local residents who acted as extras in the movie were spotlighted. Rare memorabilia was displayed, and in keeping with the theme of *Easy Rider*, a hog rally of Harley Davidson bikers was hosted. A hog rally has nothing to do with swine. Rather, it's an acronym, HOG, meaning the Harley Owners Group. Proceeds from Morganza's anniversary event were used to benefit the restoration of Morganza High School, a historic building from the 1940s that has been vacant since 2008 and is in need of repair.

On the main drag of town is a combo bait shop/convenience store gas station/bakery/sit-down café called Spillway Café. It's become a magnet for campers, hikers, naturalists, birdwatchers (there are famous bald eagles in the region) and fishermen. Although hidden at the rear of the store, a glass case tempts with exquisite homemade cakes and pies that are as big as the moon. The small Southern café has been family owned since 2016 with a "come as you are" atmosphere. Local scenes are celebrated through pictures and artwork hung on the walls. Accent pieces use recycled wood to add a rustic feel. You can't go wrong with a menu of fried chicken, soups, amazing starters, pulled pork sandwich and poboys. The "flooded fries," a reference to the Morganza Spillway located a short distance away, includes bacon.

TEET'S FOOD MARKET

2210 WEST MAIN STREET • VILLE PLATTE, LA

Tractors line up on one side of the fancy new superstore of meats, baked goods and produce. The sweet smell of French bread and cookies baking in the shiny new kitchen travels throughout the neighborhood. The savory scents of meat cooking drift from the smokehouses. The new store faces the flagship of the old store, Teet's Food Store, Specialiste dans la Viande de Boucaniere, which means "specializing in smoked meat"—perhaps founder Lawrence "Teet" Deville is still looking on.

Nicknamed "Teet" as a derivative of petite, as he was small in stature, his hardworking days included time as a sharecropper picking cotton and driving a truck to deliver bread as he traveled dusty back roads. Armed with a skillet rather than a gun, he worked as a cook while stationed in Alaska during World War II. All of these experiences of growing up with annual family boucheries in Evangeline Parish and learning how to butcher a pig led him to open up his own general merchandise/grocery store/meat market in Ville Platte. It's a town known on the music scene for its swamp pop music, Louisiana's style of rock-and-roll.

The Town of Ville Platte, French for "flat city," was incorporated in 1858. Nearby Bayou Chicot provided the area with an abundance of natural resources of timber, leading to many sawmills being built and operated. Most folks lived on small farms and grew cotton, rice and beans in the fields and raised cattle and hogs.

Teet and his wife, Ruby, opened up their store in 1955. Twenty years later, the Devilles built a modern store across the street and expanded the fresh meat department. At one time, the town had a store on every corner. Teet's scent of swine on the racks from the smokehouse, now numbering three, draw customers in as a worthy stop-off, especially on the way to nearby Chicot State Park.

The Deville family is still at the helm. Opening the doors every day to manage the store are Chris Deville, Teet and Ruby's son, who graduated in the medical field from Louisiana State University, and third generation Luke, who graduated from the University of Louisiana–Lafayette.

At just a half-pint five-year-old, Luke began stocking shelves. A few years later, he was promoted to more responsibility after a memorable early learning experience when he walked behind the register and clumsily knocked over a slew of whiskey bottles. Luke worked at the store in various capacities during high school, but his grandpa wouldn't let him work in the meat market tables for fear he would slice off his fingers. The 4-H initiative was prominent in Ville Platte as well as FBLA (Future Business Leaders). Active in many community events, Luke recalled participating in a traditional Courir de Mardi Gras when many young men dressed in colorful tattered Mardi Gras costumes rode on trailers and visited the countryside to gather ingredients for a gumbo. Now he works the aisles like a pro, shaking hands with customers and squeezing the produce. He's involved in the local chamber of commerce, which he served as president. He's also involved in the Ville Platte downtown revitalization project.

In 2019, the Devilles followed Teet's lead and expanded the smoked meats business amid a chorus of cheers echoing from loyal customers. The ante was further raised when a superstore was built across from the 1955 store, increasing the store's footprint from five thousand square feet to twenty-one thousand square feet. More smoked meats are prepared with the smokehouses, each accommodating 1,200 pounds of sausage and 120 pounds of tasso. The smokehouse is fired up daily and organized with top racks of sausage and bottom racks for offal like tails, hocks, pig feet and neck bones. A mix of woods like red oak, pecan and hickory, when available, are used, while the logs are checked every fifteen minutes in the early stage of the smoking to fill the air with an intoxicating aroma.

The motto "Specialiste dans la Viande Boucanee" is posted at the entrance of the new store, as is a picture of Teet as a testament to the founder who had foresight to take a chance on building a business from scratch. Many requests for smoked meats are turned in. Among them is Teet's signature ponce, a pig's stomach that has been stuffed with pork sausage, followed by a monitored smoking for several hours. The smoked ponce can be further cooked as a roast, either in the oven or on a stovetop in the same way in which a roast is prepared. The secret to preparing ponce is slow cooking the hunk of pork, as it is a recognized technique in cooking many Cajun dishes. When slow cooked, the meat becomes tender, just right for slicing and serving on rice in a sea of gravy. You can also reheat leftover ponce and pile it up between two slices of bread to make a Cajun sandwich. Promotional T-shirts are on display, giving Teet's a chance to brag about its ponce with a humorous tag of "Peace, Love and Ponce."

A larger meat counter and processing area, as headed by Chris Deville, were added, as was high-tech equipment such as sausage stuffers. This ensures that the process of boudin making and sausage is more efficient, though still using Teet's original recipes. One of the oldest meat markets in Evangeline Parish, this tempting candy store of smoked meats offers a vast variety: smoked ham hocks, stuffed picnic heart, stuffed and seasoned quail and sausage combinations any way you can imagine. Chris Deville's day begins at dawn.

For thirty years Chris worked hard beside his late father, Teet, who passed away in 2015, and learned what it means to put your heart and soul into what you love. Though Chris put in his time to be a dedicated leader, he never forgot about putting family first. Waking up in the early morning hours to go to work is easier knowing you are doing what is best for your family's future. Chris still makes Teet's Famous Hogshead cheese using the same method and recipe his father passed on to him. Though the location has changed, the quality and service have not.

For those in a rush for lunch or dinner, a fancy buffet counter of plate lunch entrées has been added for easy pickup of smothered pork dishes and rice and gravy. Look out for the smoky tasso and fresh turkey wings on special occasions. A variety of black iron pots and big spoons for cooking are displayed in the cookware section, along with favorite Cajun seasonings of Slap Ya Mama, Kary's Roux and Jack Miller's BBQ Sauce, all prized essentials that originated in Ville Platte.

Once in a while, Teet's goes on the road when Luke participates in community cook-offs such as the Smoked Meats Festival in Ville Platte and the Swine Festival in Basile. His team focuses on cooking smoked tasso roast and other dishes. Tasso is Cajun ham made from the pork shoulder, cured in salt and heavily spiced and smoked. Among the dishes he and teammate Justin Lafleur have created for other events are the impressive "ponce bombs" in which the meat (pig stomach stuffed with sausage) is cut into chunks. It's layered with pineapple slices and wrapped in bacon with cream cheese and jalapeño. The quirky dish is cooked on the barbecue pit until done. Leave it to the Ville Platte boys to hatch an unexpected creation for camp cookouts. Their crazy Texas Twinkies are jalapeño peppers stuffed with shredded brisket and cream cheese; they then wrap the cylinders with bacon and set them on the pit.

Teet's also proudly participates in Le Grand Hoorah, a celebration of Cajun and Creole culture begun in 2015 that introduces French music, dancing, crafts and even a Saturday morning boucherie, drawing in folks from around the globe. The spring event kicks off the Dewey Balfa Cajun and Creole Heritage Week at Chicot State Park.

THIB'S BOUDIN AND CRACKLIN HOUSE

429 SOUTH BULLARD STREET • OPELOUSAS, LA

Frank Thibodeaux is slap-happy about cooking. During football season, he dedicates Sunday afternoons to whipping up a big pot of something savory to feed his entourage of cousins as they watch the New Orleans Saints football game. It's likely there will be friendly squabbles about whether the gumbo is ready to be served. Chances are good that much yelling at the TV will happen if the referee makes a bad call during the football game.

The building that houses the meat market has a red-brick front façade and bright yellow siding. Fifty years ago, it was the site of a record store. Music blasted through city blocks as wax records were played. For a span of twenty years, the building was vacant before being converted to a meat market under a previous owner.

Meanwhile, in Germany, Opelousas native Frank Thibodeaux introduced fellow soldiers to the richness of Cajun cuisine by making boudin while he served in the U.S. Army. The kitchen skills he learned growing up followed him throughout his twenty-year military career, which carried him all over the world. Thibodeaux grew up with a large family, as both of his parents had numerous siblings, and his neighborhood hosted a boucherie every autumn. He recalled that every bit of the pig was used to create a dish. He helped out by learning the fine art of frying crackling when he was eight years old.

Another dish he learned how to cook from his mother was chitterlings. This dish uses the pig's intestines as the main ingredient. It has a reputation for its pungent order while it's boiling on the stove. Frank has a trick or two up his sleeve. Rather than using vinegar as an additive to the chitterlings, he adds potato chunks along with onions and bell pepper, a block of margarine and chili peppers. He stands back patiently and sets the pot to cooking for three hours.

In the back of Frank's mind, when his military time was coming to an end, he recalled his love for his Cajun roots and decided to return to his hometown. His joy of interacting with folks, along with a deep-rooted passion for cooking, convinced him to take over a small neighborhood meat market business in 2013.

Frank is well versed in making boudin and frying "lightweight" crackling, made of pig fat and skin. Coolers are stocked with specialty smoked meats such as smoked turkey necks, which he ranks high as a tasty addition to gumbo, tasso and pork chops. The smokehouse behind the store is always smoldering, all set for the meats that customers request for plate lunches. Every Sunday there's finger-licking barbecue ribs, Wednesdays are for pig feet and tripe to fill you up, and Thursdays are for smothered pork neck bone with rice and gravy.

On occasion, while the pots are cooking the sides of mustard greens and corn maque choux, you may catch Frank busy stirring a Dutch oven for

Boudin—it's what's for breakfast. *Courtesy of St. Landry Parish Tourist Commission.*

some home cooking of raccoon stew. This is definitely not on Thib's plate lunch menu.

Every July, Frank's cousins psych up to compete in the Cousins' Hen Cook-Off. The rules are simple: the dish has to include "rice and gravy" and be full of flavor with just the right touch of seasoning. Frank's wild card of a secret weapon is the ninety-weight gravy he makes that is thick enough that a spoon can stand up in it.

WATERMARK SALOON

103 Main Street • Columbia, LA 71418

There's a little town in North Louisiana, one that doesn't roll up the sidewalks at night.

Columbia, parish seat of Caldwell Parish, was visited by Spanish explorer Hernando de Soto in the mid-1500s as he traveled down the Ouachita River. The town was later settled by a variety of European settlers and became prosperous as a steamboat town. Farmers brought in cotton, timber and other commodities to ship to New Orleans via the Ouachita River. Once a bustling riverboat town, this trading post experienced a downturn in growth once the railroad was built in the region in 1888. The town also experienced hardships with a yellow fever epidemic in 1856 and a major fire in 1876 destroying a majority of the homes. With rebuilding and revitalization efforts, the town has stayed small with an inviting atmosphere.

Don't miss the scenic attributes of the town. Plan to stop and take some time to visit some of the old churches and houses. Hang out to enjoy one of the festivals, and take advantage of hunting deer, rabbit, quail and turkey. The charming downtown was developed primarily by entrepreneurial Italian immigrants over one hundred years ago. The Watermark Saloon is a popular stop for visitors as well as locals after enjoying a stroll on the adjacent river walk to enjoy spectacular views. The name of the tavern comes from the display of a knee-high high-water line from the Great Flood of 1927.

As the oldest saloon on the Ouachita River, the spunky two-story brick building was originally known as the Ticheli Building and dates to 1918. The upstairs once served as living quarter, but the downstairs was always a neighborhood bar. The woodsy, comfortable setting invites camaraderie through the pool table and big-screen TV set to regional sports games.

Scene from picturesque cemetery in Columbia, Louisiana. *Courtesy of Schepis Museum.*

Pressed tin ceilings and brick walls along with memorabilia relating to riverboat days lend a New Orleans atmosphere, though in a quieter setting. Dropping by for a beer and ongoing domino games may lead to staying in to listen to live music or enjoying home cooking during weekly steak nights or special events in which red beans and rice, jambalaya or gumbo are served.

A lot of history is packed into this little town, which was the site of a Civil War skirmish. There are a couple of beautifully restored old houses and churches. A highlight is the picturesque Cemetery on the Hill, where the winding path leads you to the top. Along the way are blooms of azaleas and dogwood trees and changing leaves in autumn. Ornate angel statues and wrought-iron gates, as well as unique grave markers, make the ride or walk worth visiting.

WORD OF MOUTH CAFE

918 Foisy Street • Alexandria, LA

From the outside, you might skip this unpretentious café as you beat the sidewalks in downtown Alexandria, past the courthouse and a couple of law firms.

It's situated in a cozy white house with a front porch stoop. The front door is painted bright red, which in some cultures means "Welcome." The regular lunch bunch of customers enjoys off-the-chart fresh dishes in an inviting atmosphere.

Once inside, two dining rooms are decorated with colorful artwork along with a vintage fishing lure collection. Plenty of plate lunches head out the door. Standing in line gives you time to skim through the day's specials, all written on chalkboards.

Owner/Chef John Gunter is fearless with his blend of spices to make every dish sizzle, whether it's the delicious soups, salads, tacos with spicy shredded pork and grilled onions or other dishes he creates. His self-proclaimed goal is to make taste buds tingle. Surrender to the scoop of yummy bread pudding included with all of the specials. Scrumptious pulled hot-pressed pork and Cuban sandwiches are popular. Foodies love to take "Camera Eats First" pics of the amazing ahi tuna salad to share on social media. If you've had a rough weekend with a hectic schedule or your favorite football team lost, the café offers something to look forward to. Mondays mean the comfort food special of red beans and rice. Words like *delish* spread in light-hearted whispering among the diners when he serves chicken and sausage jambalaya on frosty days.

The chef's father operated a Baton Rouge diner during the late 1960s in which Gunter was introduced to the culinary arts. Word of Mouth Cafe debuted in 2010 and is open for weekday lunches only. And most customers learn about this little gem of a lunch spot through word of mouth.

7

TREASURED HEIRLOOMS TO ACCOMPANY PORCINE DISHES

CAMELLIA BEANS

NEW ORLEANS, LA

Red beans and rice is a simple dish that's served as a strapping comfort food. Just let it simmer for hours and check on it occasionally. It can be prepared without meat, though ingenious Cajun cooks like to throw in ham hocks, smoked sausage, andouille, bacon fat or even a smoked piggy tail.

How was the weekday of Monday tagged as the traditional day to prepare this popular Louisiana dish? Often in Louisiana households, a Sunday lunch featured a platter of ham served after church services. If there was a ham bone left over, it could be used to flavor red beans and rice on the following day.

On Sunday night, the homemaker soaked dried red beans in water overnight. Early Monday, a trinity of onions, bell pepper and celery was chopped. A big pot was prepared to add beans and meats. The simmering on the stove began until the beans were tender and started to thicken. As the delicious smell filled the house, the cook occasionally checked and sampled the dish while undertaking the long haul of running a household. A common household chore on Monday was doing the laundry. In older days, this was done by hand using homemade soap made from pig lard and scents. Scrubbing shirts, dresses and other articles of clothing was done by hand. Once rinsed and fed through a hand-cranked ringer, the damp clothes were hung on an outdoor clothesline to dry. Depending on the size of the household, this process could prove tedious. Other tasks to keep the household running efficiently included mending torn clothes as people were frugal and extended the life of what they wore. Barnyard chickens were fed, and eggs were plucked from nesting spots. The cook budgeted her time to bake an afternoon cornbread in a cast-iron skillet. The honey cornbread complemented the spiciness of the red beans and rice.

The chosen beans used for the classic Monday dish of red beans and rice are kidney beans, which originated in Peru. As people migrated to other countries for opportunity, these beans were carried over to America and served as an important protein source. The Caribbean version of our Creole red beans and rice, which is considered a staple in Latin and Caribbean households, often includes the addition of coconut milk. The vegetarian version is often served as a side dish to accompany a chicken entrée.

With an ambitious plan of starting a cotton business, Sawyer Hayward moved from West Indies to New Orleans in 1850. His son Lucius "L.H." Hayward, now the company namesake, recognized the opportunity of sourcing beans and other produce as well as dry good commodities in New Orleans's French Market. As the city population grew with more immigrants, the demand for specific commodities such as beans increased. As Lucius's attention focused more on beans, he studied the versatility and health benefits. In 1923, his son, Gordon Hayward, dedicated a company to this legume, proclaiming the enterprise Camellia Beans in honor of the favorite flower of his mother.

The company remains a faithful fixture in New Orleans and is family-owned through four generations, descended from Sawyer Hayward. Although red kidney beans are the reigning star of the company's basket of products, the variety has expanded to include black-eyed peas, lentils, lima beans and more.

Give a shout out to New Orleans for celebrating everything, including creating a festival or, in this case, a Mardi Gras krewe dedicated to red beans. The Krewe of Red Beans was founded in 2008 by Devin DeWulf when he was inspired to go all out for an unusual Halloween costume in 2008, a bean-covered suit. The following year, a "bean parade" was hosted on Lundi Gras, which is the Monday before Mardi Gras. Every year, the krewe of 150 members schemes about crazier antics and elaborately beaded and feathered costumes to celebrate the delicious red bean.

There are many fans of the creamy red beans and rice, including native New Orleanian and musical icon Louis Armstrong. So important was this homemade dish that he had a test before he proposed marriage to his future wife, Lucille, a native New Yorker. Louis requested that she cook this classic dish for him and include his favorite pork ingredients of salt pork or bacon. Later in life, Louis ended his correspondence with "Red Beans and Ricely Yours" as a salutation.

CHISESI'S
New Orleans, LA

Louisiana has often been compared to the famous dish of gumbo with its eclectic blend of spices and other ingredients. Many cultures have made us all the richer by sharing their folkways through music, arts and cuisine. Playing an integral role in Louisiana's culture, the Italians immigrated to Louisiana in the late 1800s. They arrived at the Port of New Orleans after fleeing from their homeland in search of a better life by bravely facing an unknown land. Many found work on sugar plantations, taking over duties from newly freed slaves. Some became farmers, while others opened fruit and vegetable stands that later transitioned to corner stores.

The Chisesi family bravely trekked across the Atlantic Ocean by ship. Their enterprise began by setting up a business in New Orleans. They raised chickens, ducks and rabbits, caging and loading them in a truck for transportation to the French Quarter to peddle their wares. After a promising start, they upgraded to a business on Lapeyrouse Street in New Orleans that prospered even during the Great Depression. Always ready to take a chance, they began selling wholesale and retail live poultry.

Family owned for over one hundred years, Chisesi's has been an iconic provision of New Orleans through four generations within the same family. The whimsical logo of a little pig represents the variety of ham products it produces.

When Hurricane Katrina hit New Orleans on August 29, 2005, the future of Chisesi's was nearly wiped out. The company faced severe challenges, as the factory located near the Superdome was severely damaged and power was out for an extended time. There were over two million pounds of spoiled meat in the walk-in coolers that had to be cleaned out. Although dispirited with thoughts of throwing in the towel and permanently shutting down the business, the Chisesi leaders maintained faith in their staff and the City of New Orleans. A course of action was devised. They wouldn't give

Right: Family owned for over one hundred years, Chisesi's is an icon of New Orleans. *Courtesy of Chisesi's.*

Below: Early general store of Chisesi's. *Courtesy of Chisesi's.*

Leave it to New Orleans to host the world's biggest po'boy with Chisesi's ham. *Courtesy of Chisesi's.*

up; instead, the roof of the building would be repaired, and the structure would be refurbished to recapture a sense of normalcy. Miraculously, Chisesi's reopened for business only two weeks before Thanksgiving, one of the busiest times of the year for slicing hams at the family table.

The business continues to grow, with expansion to a new facility on Jefferson Highway. A Cajun ham was recently introduced that steals the show. It pairs two Louisiana staples: Tony Chachere Creole seasoning is injected into a Chisesi ham. Other Southern-style smoked meat products include rope smoked sausage, sliced roast beef, smoked whole ham, chorizo and Italian sausage.

"Lunch is on us" on National Sandwich Day, the first Sunday in November in New Orleans. Everyone is invited to sample a slice of the world's biggest poboy, measuring five hundred feet long. On hand are the collaborators to make Louisiana's signature sandwich, the poboy, as it's sliced, diced, piled high with meat and freely shared to feed the masses. For four years, Chisesi Brothers, Leidenheimer Baking Company, Blue Plate Mayonnaise and Parkway Bakery have united in building a killer poboy. Curious onlookers line up to wolf down the tasty treat of the wacky sandwich, which takes over a whole city block. And adding a musical performance by the Storyville Stomper brass band makes it a party. The eats are free, though donations to end hunger and homelessness are accepted.

EVANGELINE MAID BREAD

LAFAYETTE, LA

A hot and messy plate lunch of smothered pork needs a finishing touch, such as a slice of snow-white bread atop a heated mound of rice and gravy. The soft white bread of choice for southwest Louisiana has been Evangeline Maid for over one hundred years.

The doors of the bakery famous for this iconic Cajun bread were opened in Youngsville in 1919 by the Huval family. Founder Joe Huval first donned the apron when he baked bread while serving in the U.S. Army during World War II. When he returned home from France after the war, he used his fifty-dollar military service bonus as well as a small loan from a sympathetic dentist to open the small bakery he named Huval Baking Company. He refined his bread recipe and delivered fresh loaves house to house for five cents a loaf. To expand the business, he purchased a small existing bakery near downtown Lafayette in 1926 and merged the facilities.

Since the wholesome bread debuted, the image of Evangeline that graces bread wrappers and advertisements has only been upgraded twice since it was created. The persona of a lovely young lady dressed in blue is tied to Henry Wadsworth Longfellow's 1847 epic story about Acadian lovers Evangeline and Gabriel. Separated during the Acadian exile from Canada, Evangeline died of a broken heart.

In branding the look of his Evangeline Maid label, Huval selected his daughter Mary to pose. She was nineteen years old when she modeled for the illustration, never imaging how far-reaching her image would travel. She has adorned millions of bread packages and advertising specialties such as pencils, neckties, hair combs and matchboxes. Mary Helen Huval Gucherau died in 2011 at age ninety-two.

To bolster business opportunities, Lafayette businessman Frem F. Boustany Sr. purchased a 50 percent share of Huval Baking Company in 1947. In 1976, Flower Industries, now Flowers Foods, acquired the baking company and expanded beyond the Evangeline Maid label by adding brands such as Nature's Own, Cobblestone and Country Hearth with everything from honey wheat, whole grain and hamburger buns.

Baking bread at home can be compared to a science experiment. Precise measurements of the basic combination of yeast, flour, sugar, salt, oil and water to make the dough rise properly are critical. Whether baking bread at home or in a commercial bakery, the main processes include mixing and

A messy rice and gravy lunch has been topped with Evangeline Maid bread of Lafayette for over one hundred years. *Courtesy of Annette Huval.*

kneading, proofing, baking and cooling, and every step is equally important to wind up with a perfect loaf.

In a commercial bakery, everything works on a grander scale. Rather than a small mixer, the dough has to be processed through a one-thousand-pound mixer, a splitter that precisely slices loaves into slices and giant proofing chambers.

Over 100,000 loaves are baked daily. They slide through four levels of a huge oven. Once de-panned, the loaves cool off as they slowly travel one-third of a mile on an overhead conveyor belt. This mesmerizing scene is similar to watching a model train chugging along as it turns curves. Once the loaves cool down to one hundred degrees, they progress to automated slicing and packing into bread bags.

To commemorate the 100th anniversary of the famous Cajun brand, a mural was painted on the bakery's exterior walls to represent the three images of Evangeline Maid through the years, with founder Joe Huval proudly looking over. And the iconic billboard with a giant revolving loaf of Evangeline Maid bread, which dates back to the 1960s, continues to thrill fans of roadside attractions as they drive on Simcoe Street in Lafayette.

FALCON RICE

CROWLEY, LA

What's it like to have an evening meal around the campfire without a steaming mound of fluffy rice to drop into a gumbo? This popular mainstay plays an important role in many of our Cajun dishes.

In colonial America, rice farming was prevalent in the Carolinas and Georgia. After the Civil War, labor changes and challenges and damages to crops from numerous hurricanes stilted the industry. Opportunity for cultivating rice fields transitioned farther south.

This area of Louisiana, blessed with wet marshes and low-lying prairieland, contributed an ideal landscape for rice production. Rice fields transitioned westward from the Louisiana banks of the Mississippi River to the Cajun prairies. Property proved to be cheaper, and with the building of a railroad in the works, opportunity appeared to be on the horizon. Other cultures, in addition to the Acadians, settled in southwest Louisiana. Germans also established communities such as Roberts Cove and Crowley in Acadia Parish, recognizing the prospects for growing rice as a livelihood. They also had the foresight to modernize harvesting and milling methods.

With the development of rice mills in Crowley, the town became known as the Rice Capital of the World and hosted its first celebration through a 1927 Rice Carnival. Ten years later, the first International Rice Festival was held in October to commemorate the town's golden jubilee, making it the largest and oldest agricultural festival in Louisiana.

Along with the prosperity of rice farming for this valued crop, these same rice fields could be used for a second purpose that was high in demand—harvesting crawfish. The majority of crawfish was harvested from the Atchafalaya Basin at one time. Trial and error proved that the rice fields of the Cajun prairieland could be adapted to expand the aquaculture industry. Because of the idolization of crawfish and all of the beloved crawfish dishes, rice farmers discovered astounding possibilities for commercial harvest.

Rice season from planting to harvesting takes place from March to July. During cooler temperatures in September, crawfish ponds are flooded and the crawfish are rice-fed. Harvesting for crawfish begins in December and continues through June. And the year-round cycle of rice to crawfish continues.

Today, Louisiana ranks as the third-largest rice producer in the United States. Americans eat approximately thirty pounds of rice per person annually, especially as the popularity of sushi has increased. Not surprisingly,

Falcon Rice of Crowley, begun in 1942. *Courtesy of Falcon Rice.*

Louisianans enjoy double that amount, likely because of the Cajun dishes that include the basic grain, making its addition a perfect balance to the thick, meaty broth of gumbo.

One of the oldest rice businesses in Crowley was begun by the Falcon family in Crowley in 1942 when Edward and Evelyn Falcon collaborated with area farmers to purchase rough rice. They planned to clean, treat and resell it for

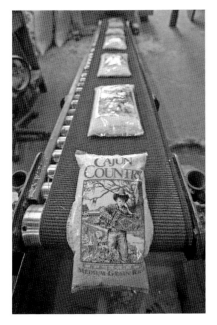

So many Louisiana dishes use rice as a key ingredient. *Courtesy of Falcon Rice.*

seed in time for spring planting. The couple bought the property to build a mill through a 1938 tax sale for $19.19. Falcon Rice Mill installed a million-dollar operation during the 1950s, producing several brands to include a variety of long, medium, whole-grain brown, jasmine and popcorn rice to suit many tastes.

The third generation of the Falcons, siblings Robert and Christine Trahan, along with their spouses, oversee the many facets of taking the virgin rice and transforming it into the popular staple of our Cajun and Creole dishes.

The front porch of Falcon Rice Mill has rocking chairs to welcome visitors. Group tours are hosted, and folks are amazed by all the bells and whistles of sorters, thrashers, robotic arms for lifting pallets and automated packaging. The plant runs five days a week year-round thanks to fifty dedicated employees who produce a variety of labels. The busiest season is usually autumn, as consumers prepare for colder weather and the holiday season, when they may indulge with rice-based dishes. Falcon prepares rice in bags from twelve ounces up to fifty kilos. It produces several brands, such as Toro long grain and Cajun Country, and has diversified to outturn rice that appeals to Asian and Spanish markets. Rice bran is the brown layer on the rice inside the hull and is a byproduct of the milling process. Falcon Rice Mill sells brokens to dog food manufacturers. Bran is sold to feed lots for cattle, and hulls may be used for bedding for horses and cattle.

Many have asked if the family has ties to Cajun musical legend Joe Falcon and his wife, Cleoma, who recorded "Allons a Lafayette" in 1928, the first Cajun French song recorded. Joe Falcon, of Spanish descent, was especially renowned for his mastery of playing the accordion, while Cleoma was famous for her guitar picking and singing. The couple released forty-five titles. Joe Falcon was Falcon Rice Mill founder Edward Falcon's cousin. Accordions have stayed in the family, as Randy Falcon, second generation of Falcon Rice Mill, continues to build custom instruments.

FARM FRESH FOOD SUPPLIERS, INC.
MATT & DANA

Amite, LA

Rather than gifting the traditional fruitcake to family at Christmas, why not go a little wilder? Imagine the thrill when you surprise your folks with a jar of pickled pig lips.

It's not for the faint of heart! At first glance, the concoction resembles those unforgettable mysterious jars in high school biology lab. The jar of pickled pig parts is filled with a fluid that resembles red Kool-Aid but is actually a vinegary liquid. It's blended with salt and other spices that are tinged with red dye to add a tangy taste to the pork bits. Pickling meat as a way to preserve and store food has been an Acadian staple for hundreds of years.

This beloved and sometimes misunderstood Southern snack food may present an amusing intro to start up a conversation about unique foods. Pig lips are all meat, as they are trimmed of fat. The chunks receive high praise for their appealing texture and strong porky flavor. Fans of this appetizing choice of pickled delight often enjoy by pairing it with the savory snack of potato chips. Roll the rosy lips in a bag of crushed potato chips to add some crunchiness. This irresistible meaty hunk will be added to your grocery list for special occasions.

Pig lips are only one of the trove of goodies that has been produced by Matt & Dana brand since the early 1930s. As blues singer Bessie Smith sang, "Gimme a pig foot and a bottle of beer." The Southern delicacy of a pig foot stems from European medieval times when cooks used pig trotters (their term for pig feet) and pickled them to serve as an appetizer before a feast. Customers suggest that the best way to eat pigs' feet is straight from the jar. The flavor may be complemented with a cold mug of brew. Only the front feet of the pig, without the hoof attached, are used to produce pickled feet. They are sized approximately five inches long, with bone in.

Matt & Dana incorporates a centuries-old recipe for pickling pig lips and feet, eggs, sausage and pork hocks. This Amite, Louisiana company has been overseen by three generations of the Dufour family.

It began with Rosemond Dufour, who grew up in Avoyelles Parish, Louisiana, where French was his first language. He was introduced to English while in grade school and, like many other students, was disciplined for speaking French in the classroom.

Pickled pig's feet are a Southern tradition. *Courtesy of Matt and Dana.*

As a young man, Dufour moved to New Orleans seeking employment; he admitted that he "didn't want to spend his life picking cotton" in cotton-rich Avoyelles Parish. He started a meatpacking business and sidelined through the years by selling various food items and sundries he pulled from his car trunk. A key item were the jars of pig feet from local producers that he peddled. His son Lionel regularly made the rounds of the sales route with his dad to visit bars and markets. During the 1950s, Rosemond recognized that pig feet and pig lips had become high-demand snacks. He was convinced to produce his own brand.

Since inception of the business, leadership has transitioned to Rosemond's sons Lionel and Roland John Dufour. Today, the specialty establishment is run by third generation Matt Dufour. Plans are that their children will continue operating the business, making it a fourth generation overseeing pickled pig parts.

While Matt was growing up, he was not allowed to play hooky from school, except on rare occasions. He was thrilled to accompany his father to an annual national meatpacking convention in Chicago because this related to the family livelihood and was considered an educational outing. Matt also shadowed his father as Lionel met with suppliers in the Northern states to discuss the specific cuts that were needed to produce the best pickled pig products in the United States.

The company employs fifty workers in-house. Over two hundred outside salespeople spread the word of the unique products, which are distributed throughout the United States. The family-focused business sells its products mainly to convenience stores and wholesalers. The jars of bright pig feet are often spotted near cash registers in roadside gas stations. Some supermarkets dedicate more shelf space to Matt & Dana's pickled pig products than they do cans of tuna.

No slaughterhouse is located on the compound of company Farm Fresh Suppliers Inc. in Amite. Rather, a stream of eighteen-wheeler trucks deliver iced cases of various pig parts to the factory. There was a time when other products were produced, and the market was tested for consumption of pork ears, jaws, tails and tongues. However, the top seller remains the exceptional Southern treasure of pig feet.

Connoisseurs of savory treats enjoy the pickled morsels by reaching into a jar and pulling out a meaty hunk. However, many other products, such as the smoked sausage, can be used to add flavor to soups and stews. These unique pickled products have garnered national attention through episodes of Food Network and Discovery Channel programs.

RECIPES

Teet's Duck and Sausage Fajitas
Courtesy of Teet's Food Store, Ville Platte

4 duck breasts
Fajita seasoning
2 tablespoons vegetable oil
½ pound Teet's Smoked Jalapeño Sausage, coined
½ red bell pepper, sliced
½ yellow bell pepper, sliced
½ green bell pepper, sliced
1 red onion, sliced
1 yellow onion, sliced
Tortillas
Sour cream, jalapeños, Sriracha sauce (optional)

Fajita Seasoning
2 tablespoons chili powder
1 tablespoon salt
1 tablespoon paprika
1 ½ teaspoons onion powder
1 teaspoon garlic powder
1 ½ teaspoons cayenne pepper
¼ teaspoon crushed red pepper flakes
1 teaspoon cumin

Season whole duck breasts with fajita seasoning and refrigerate for at least 30 minutes. In a skillet, preferably cast iron, add oil, and heat to medium heat, then brown sausage and vegetables. Once browned, remove from skillet. Heat skillet to medium-high heat, add whole duck breasts and cook until medium rare, 3–5 minutes on each side. Once done, remove skillet from heat and remove breasts from skillet. Slice into strips on cutting board. Add meat, sausage, onions, and peppers back into skillet and serve. Place in tortillas and add toppings as desired.

•　•　•

Sausage and Smothered Potatoes
Courtesy of Johnson's Boucanniere

1 pound Johnson's smoked sausage, cut or sliced (any flavor will work well)
1 medium onion, diced
2 cloves garlic, minced
½ green bell pepper, diced
2 pounds red potatoes, peeled and cut
Enough water or broth to barely cover the sausage and potatoes
Johnson's seasoning to taste
Diced green onion

Start by browning your sausage. When you have fried down the sausage, it will leave drippings in the pan and will start to brown on the bottom of the pan. Add the onion, garlic and bell pepper and allow to cook down until they begin to brown. Add the potatoes and broth. Sprinkle seasoning over the dish to your own taste. Cover and allow to cook on low to medium heat approximately one hour or one and a half hours. Stir about every 20 minutes or so to prevent sticking and to help the potatoes break up into the gravy. Add green onion and stir in right before serving. May be served over rice.

•　•　•

RECIPIES

Pork Chops with Lima Beans
Courtesy of "Louisiana's Cajun Bayou"

6 pork chops
¼ cup oil
1 cup chopped onion
2 ribs celery, chopped
4 cloves garlic, diced
2 tablespoons flour
2 cups water
3 cans lima beans (A 16-ounce package frozen lima beans may be used in place of canned beans)

Brown pork chops in heavy oiled pot. Remove and set aside. Add onion, celery and garlic, stirring until slightly brown. Sprinkle flour over mixture, stirring constantly. Slowly add 2 cups water. Add chops and lima beans. Cover and continue cooking until chops are tender. Serve with rice.

• • •

Bittersweet Plantation Sugar-Cured Smokehouse Ham
Courtesy of Chef John Folse

Prep time: 24 hours
Yields: 1 (12–15 pound) ham
Most local butcher supply companies sell Art's Brown Sugar Cure as well as cheesecloth suitable for smoking hams. One of my favorite suppliers is Targil Seasoning & Butcher Supply in Opelousas, Louisiana.

1 (1½-pound) bag Art's Brown Sugar Cure
3 gallons cold water
1 cup brown sugar, divided
1½ cups Louisiana cane syrup, divided
1 (8–10 pound) shank-on wild boar or pork leg
¼ cup cracked black pepper
Pecan wood or hickory chips for flavoring

In a 5-gallon pot or plastic pail, blend brown sugar cure, water, ½ cup brown sugar and ¾ cup cane syrup. Whisk together thoroughly. Using a large meat syringe, inject ham on each side (in 6–10 places) with cure mixture. Ham must be injected with an amount of cure equivalent to 10 percent of the weight of the ham. Place ham in remaining cure (brine) and allow to marinate 36 hours. Preheat smokehouse or home-style smoker to 120°F. When ready to cook, remove ham from brine and pat dry. Create a rub using remaining sugar, syrup and black pepper. Coat ham thoroughly with rub and then place in a cheesecloth or "ham sock." Place ham in preheated smokehouse. Add pecan wood or hickory chips and cook until internal temperature of ham reaches 175°F. (Add more wood or chips as necessary during the cooking process to maintain smoke.) Remove ham and cool at room temperature 6–8 hours prior to refrigeration. Serve hot or chilled. Ham may also be frozen for later use.

• • •

Butter Beans with Pickled Pork or Smoked Ham Hocks
Courtesy of Camellia Beans

Yield: 8 servings

1 (1-pound) package Camellia-brand large lima beans
2 tablespoons vegetable oil
1 pound pickled pork or smoked ham hocks
1 large onion, chopped
4 cloves garlic, chopped
2 quarts water
2 bay leaves
Salt, pepper and hot sauce, to taste
Hot cooked rice
Hot buttered French bread

Rinse and sort beans. (Optional: Soak beans using your preferred method.) Heat oil in a large pot over medium-high heat. If using pickled pork, add to pot; sauté 5 minutes or until browned. Add onions and garlic; sauté 5–10 minutes. Add 2 quarts water, bay leaves and, if using, smoked ham hocks. Bring to a boil. Add beans and stir well. Return to a low boil; cover, reduce heat to low and simmer 2 to 2½ hours, or until beans are soft and creamy, stirring occasionally. Adjust seasonings to taste with salt, pepper and hot sauce. Serve over hot cooked rice with buttered French bread.

•　•　•

Rabbit and Smoked Pork Sausage Sauce Piquante
Courtesy of Chef John Folse

Prep Time: 2–2½ hours
Yields: 8 Servings
Sauce piquante, or "peppery sauce," is a stew-like dish of French origin in Louisiana. It can be made with seafood, domesticated meats or wild game. Tomato is added to the dish to give it a slight rusty color.

1 cup oil
1 rabbit, dressed and cut into 8 pieces
Salt and black pepper to taste
Cayenne pepper to taste
1 pound smoked pork sausage, sliced
1 cup flour
1 cup chopped onions
1 cup chopped celery
¼ cup minced red bell pepper
¼ cup minced green bell pepper
¼ cup minced yellow bell pepper
2 tablespoons diced garlic
1 (6-ounce) can tomato paste
1 (10-ounce) can Rotel®
1 quart beef stock
1 tablespoon sugar
2 tablespoons Worcestershire sauce
2 tablespoons minced basil leaves
1 tablespoon fresh thyme leaves
½ cup sliced green onions
¼ cup chopped parsley

1 pinch red pepper flakes
Steamed white rice for serving

In a heavy-bottomed Dutch oven, heat oil over medium-high heat. Season rabbit using salt, black pepper and cayenne pepper. Sauté rabbit until golden brown, stirring occasionally. Remove from oil and keep warm. Add sausage to pot and sauté 5–7 minutes or until lightly brown. Remove from oil and keep warm. Add flour to oil in pot, and using a wire whisk, stir constantly until a dark brown roux is achieved. Add onions, celery, bell peppers and garlic. Sauté 3–5 minutes or until vegetables are wilted. Add tomato paste and continue to stir 5–6 minutes or until the sauce is a nice brown color. Add Rotel® and beef stock. Blend well into the roux mixture, bring to a rolling boil and reduce to simmer. Add rabbit, sausage, sugar, salt and peppers. Blend well. Add Worcestershire, basil and thyme. Allow to simmer 1 hour and check rabbit for tenderness. An additional 30 minutes may be needed for simmering, depending on age of rabbit. Once rabbit is tender, finish with green onions, parsley and red pepper flakes. Serve hot over a plate of steamed white rice.

• • •

Bourgeois Boudin Stuffed Bell Peppers
Courtesy of Bourgeois Meat Market, Thibodaux, LA

Large bell peppers
Bourgeois White Boudin (or even better, Bourgeois Crawfish Boudin)
Breadcrumbs
Note: You will need one pound of boudin per large bell pepper

Preheat oven to 350 degrees. Cut bell peppers in half long ways and clean them out. Take boudin out of the casing and stuff into the bell peppers. Sprinkle breadcrumbs on top and put into the oven for about 2 hours or until bell peppers are at desired softness.

• • •

Caribbean Pork Tenderloin

Courtesy of Susan Ford, publisher of Louisiana Kitchen & Culture *magazine*

Yield: Serves 4

1 ½ pounds pork tenderloin, trimmed

1 8-ounce can pineapple in its own juice (not heavy syrup), drained, juice reserved
½ cup pineapple juice
¼ cup soy sauce, Tamari preferred
1 teaspoon ground cumin
4 cloves garlic, coarsely chopped
1–4 serrano chilis, coarsely chopped (to taste)
Juice of 1 lime
1 cup cilantro

Bring the pork tenderloin almost to room temperature in a nonreactive container or gallon-sized zip-top bag.

Place all remaining ingredients for marinade in a blender or food processor and process until finely chopped. Reserve ½ cup of marinade. Pour remaining marinade over pork tenderloin and turn to coat. Allow to rest at room temperature for at least 20 and up to 30 minutes. Meanwhile, heat a grill to medium.

Remove pork from marinade (discard marinade). Place it on the grill and cook, turning every two minutes, until internal temperature reaches 140 degrees, 12–14 minutes. The marinade that clings to the pork will brown; don't allow it to burn. When pork is done, remove to a sheet of foil large enough to make a "boat" that will enclose the loin; add reserved marinade, seal the foil tightly and allow to sit for ten minutes. Slice thinly across the grain and serve at once. Note: Serrano chilies tend to be hotter than jalapeño peppers.

•   •   •

Insta-Pot Pork Carnitas
Courtesy of Louisiana Kitchen & Culture

Yield: Serves a crowd

1 3-pound pork butt
Salt and pepper to taste
1 teaspoon cooking oil
1 ½ cups lager-style beer
1 large onion, coarsely chopped
6 cloves garlic, smashed and coarsely chopped
Coarsely chopped jalapeño or serrano pepper to taste
1 tablespoon New Mexico chili powder
1 teaspoon cumin
¾ cup fresh orange juice
1 long strip orange peel, any pith removed
½ cup fresh lime juice
1 long strip lime peel, any pith removed
2 bay leaves
1 cinnamon stick, broken into 2 to 3 pieces
1 tablespoon dried oregano, preferably Mexican

Cut pork into 2- to 3-inch pieces and sprinkle generously with salt and pepper. Set electric pressure cooker sauté setting on high. Add the oil, and working in batches, brown pork on all sides, removing to a platter as each batch is finished. If there are browned bits stuck to the bottom of the pan, add a splash of beer and scrape the pan. Add the onion, garlic and hot pepper to the rendered fat and cook, stirring often, until onion is translucent, 6 to 8 minutes. Add the chili powder and cumin and cook, stirring constantly, until very fragrant, about 1 minute (this is an important step to building flavor). Return the pork to the pan and turn pieces to coat. Add the beer, orange juice and peel, lime juice and peel, bay leaves, cinnamon stick and oregano.

Seal and set the time for 60 minutes. When the timer beeps, let pressure release naturally for 20 minutes, then vent. Using a large slotted spoon, lift out pork pieces and transfer to a rimmed baking sheet; set aside to cool. Strain the cooking liquid and discard the solids. Let the broth settle and skim off and reserve as much fat as possible; it is very flavorful. Measure ½ cup of the broth and set aside; reserve the remaining broth for another use (such as making a pot of black beans). When the pork is cool enough to handle, shred it, discarding any excess fat and gristle. Heat 2 tablespoons of the reserved fat in a large Dutch oven over medium heat; add the shredded pork and reserved ½ cup broth and cook, stirring occasionally, until broth has evaporated and pork is well browned; taste and adjust seasoning. Use carnitas to build a platter of nachos with black beans, queso, sour cream and plenty of fresh salsa. Use them to make tacos, fill burritos, tamales and enchiladas.

• • •

Cafeteria Yeast Rolls
Courtesy of Louisiana Kitchen & Culture

Yield: Makes 20 rolls

1 ½ cups warm water
1 ½ teaspoons + ⅓ cup white sugar
2 envelopes active dry yeast
2 tablespoons milk
1 egg
1 ½ teaspoons salt
5 cups all-purpose flour
2 tablespoons shortening
2 tablespoons unsalted butter, melted

Preheat oven to 400 degrees. In a large bowl, mix together the warm water and 1 ½ teaspoons sugar. Sprinkle the yeast over the top and let it stand for about 10 minutes, until the yeast is foamy. If your yeast and water mixture does not foam, your yeast may not be alive or the water was not at the correct temperature and you will have to repeat this step.

Mix the milk, egg and salt into the yeast. Measure the flour into a separate bowl, add ⅓ cup sugar and crumble the shortening into it using your fingers until it is barely noticeable. Gradually stir the flour into the wet ingredients. Mix using a wooden spoon until the dough pulls away from the sides of the bowl and starts to form a ball around the spoon. Remove the dough and knead on the counter (lightly floured) until it is a smooth consistency.

Place the dough into a well buttered or greased bowl. Metal mixing bowls help with the warmth needed for the dough to rise. Cover lightly with plastic wrap that has been buttered or sprayed with oil to prevent it from sticking to the dough. Set in a warm place to rise until the dough doubles in size. This should take about 45 minutes to 1 hour.

When the dough has risen, return it to the floured counter and knead for about 2 minutes. Let the dough rest for a few minutes, then roll out to 1 inch thick. Use a knife or pastry scraper to cut into 2-inch squares. Roll squares into balls and place into greased round pans or 11x9 baking pans, spacing about 1 inch apart. Let rise again, covered with plastic you used before, until doubled in size. You can also refrigerate the dough and let it rise overnight for baking the next day.

Bake the rolls for about 12 minutes, until golden brown. Brush the top of the rolls with melted butter as soon as they come out of the oven and serve hot.

Note: It is essential that you have a kitchen thermometer for this recipe, as you need the water at the correct temperature for the yeast to bloom—not too hot, or it will kill the yeast. The warm water this recipe calls for should be 120 to 130 degrees.

• • •

Barbecue Pork Mac and Cheese
Courtesy of Louisiana Kitchen & Culture

Yield: Serves 8

1 pound macaroni
1 pound pulled pork
1 cup barbecue sauce
1 pint heavy cream
2 teaspoons crushed garlic
2 teaspoons diced shallots
2 teaspoons fresh thyme leaves
2 cups shredded cheddar cheese (about 8 ounces)

1 tablespoon chili paste
½ cup mayonnaise
Salt and pepper to taste

For the crumb topping, combine:
1 ½ cups panko breadcrumbs
¾ cup finely grated Parmesan cheese
2 teaspoons fresh thyme leaves
½ teaspoon crushed red pepper, or to taste
1 tablespoon olive oil

Cook macaroni in a pot of generously salted boiling water until just al dente; it will finish cooking in the oven. Drain and toss with pulled pork and barbecue sauce; set aside. Combine the cream, garlic, shallots and thyme in a large saucepan over medium heat; bring to a simmer and cook, stirring often, until reduces by ¼. Whisk in the cheddar, chili paste and mayonnaise; taste, adding salt and pepper as desired. Fold cheese mixture into macaroni and pork mixture, transfer to a shallow baking dish and top with crumb topping; bake until golden and bubbly, about 40 minutes. Serve at once.

• • •

Shrimp and Pork Paella
Courtesy of Susan Ford, publisher, Louisiana Kitchen & Culture

Yield: Serves 4

3 cups chicken broth
Pinch of saffron, crumbled
1 ½ pounds pork loin, cut into ½-inch cubes
Kosher or sea salt
Olive oil
1 cup chopped onion
1 cup chopped red bell pepper
2 tablespoons chopped garlic
1 tablespoon cumin
1 tablespoon smoked paprika

½ teaspoon cayenne pepper, or to taste
1 ½ cups Arborio rice
1 cup shelled edamame or baby lima beans
2 cups baby spinach
½ cup chopped flat leaf parsley
1 dozen Louisiana shrimp, peeled and deveined

Bring the chicken broth and saffron to a bare simmer; keep warm over low heat. Preheat the oven to 400 degrees for gas, 450 for electric. Sprinkle pork with salt and toss to coat. Cover the bottom of a 13-inch paella pan or cast-iron skillet with a thin layer of olive oil. Sauté pork over high heat, stirring frequently, for 2 minutes and remove to a warm bowl. Add onion and red bell pepper to the pan and cook over medium high heat until vegetables start to soften. Add the garlic and cook until fragrant. Add the cumin, smoked paprika and cayenne pepper and stir to combine. Stir in the rice and coat well with the pan mixture. Add all the chicken broth to the pan and bring to a boil. Stir in the edamame or lima beans and pork. Reduce heat to medium low and continue to cook, stirring occasionally, until the rice mixture is no longer soupy but still has enough liquid to continue to cook. Stir in the spinach and parsley, arrange the shrimp over the top of the rice, and place in the oven. Bake until rice is just al dente, 15–20 minutes. Remove from the oven, cover the pan and let rest for 10 minutes. Serve.

BIBLIOGRAPHY

Aidells, Bruce, and Lisa Weiss. *Bruce Aidells's Complete Book of Pork*. New York: HarperCollins, 2004.

Ancelet, Barry. *Cajun Country*. Jackson: University Press of Mississippi, 1991.

Bicentennial Louisiana: Historic Sketches and Regional Recipes from the Parishes. Cultural Arts Committee, Louisiana Extension Homemakers Council, 1976.

Bosse, Alain. *The Acadian Kitchen*. Vancouver: Whitecap, 2018.

Edge, John T. *The New Encyclopedia of Southern Culture*. Chapel Hill: University of North Carolina Press, 2007.

Essig, Mark. *Lesser Beasts*. New York: Basic Books, 2015.

Fontenot, Mary Alice, and Julie Landry. *The Louisiana Experience*. Baton Rouge, LA: Claire's Publishing Division, 1983.

Gauthreaux, Alan G. *Italian Louisiana: History, Heritage and Tradition*. Charleston, SC: The History Press, 2014.

Gunderson, Mary. *Southern Plantation Cooking*. Blue Mankato, MN: Earth Books, 2000.

Herbert, Janis. *Lewis and Clark for Kids*. Chicago: Chicago Review Press, 2000.

Herbst, Ron, and Sharon Tyler Herbst. *The Deluxe Food Lover's Companion*. 2nd edition. Hauppauge, NY: Barron's Educational Series, 2015.

Johnston, Joe. *Grits to Glory, How Southern Cookin' Got So Good*. Gretna, LA: Pelican Publishing Company, 2018.

Perrin, Warren A. *Vermilion Parish*. Charleston, SC: Arcadia Publishing, 2011.

Spector, Robert. *The Mom & Pop Store: True Stories from the Heart of America*. New York: Walker & Company, 2009.

Villas, James. *Pig: King of the Southern Table*. New York: John Wiley & Sons, 2010.

Wells, Ken. *Gumbo Life; Tales from the Roux Bayou*. New York: W.W. Norton & Company, 2019.

Wilder, Laura Ingalls. *Little House in the Big Woods*. New York: HarperCollins, 1932.

ABOUT THE AUTHOR

D ixie Poché is a graduate of the University of Louisiana–Lafayette in journalism. She is a travel and corporate writer in Lafayette and author of *Classic Eateries of Cajun Country* and *Louisiana Sweets*, both published by American Palate, a division of The History Press. She enjoys doing research at the lunch counter and spends time with lots of Cajun cousins hanging out on the front porch.